101
MUST-SEE
MOVIES
FOR
GAY MEN

101
MUST-SEE
MOVIES
FOR
GAY MEN

Alonso Duralde

Advocate
BOOKS

NEW YORK

MANUFACTURED IN THE UNITED STATES OF AMERICA.

PUBLISHED BY ADVOCATE BOOKS,
AN IMPRINT OF ALYSON BOOKS,
P.O. BOX 1253, OLD CHELSEA STATION, NEW YORK, NEW YORK 10113-1251.
DISTRIBUTION IN THE UNITED KINGDOM BY TURNAROUND PUBLISHER SERVICES LTD.,
UNIT 3, OLYMPIA TRADING ESTATE, COBURG ROAD, WOOD GREEN,
LONDON N22 6TZ ENGLAND.

ISBN 0-7394-6457-4

CREDITS
COVER PHOTOGRAPHY COURTESY OF PHOTOFEST.
INTERIOR PHOTOS: *HUSTLER WHITE* (114) COURTESY STRAND RELEASING, *LIVING END* (127) COURTESY STRAND RELEASING (PHOTO BY MICHAEL MATSON), *SHOW ME LOVE* (178) COURTESY STRAND RELEASING, *SWOON* (204) COURTESY STRAND RELEASING HOME VIDEO, *ZERO PATIENCE* (242)COURTESY STRAND RELEASING HOME VIDEO.
COVER AND INTERIOR DESIGN BY AMY MARTIN.

To Suzanne for believing
and Dave for being

ACKNOWLEDGMENTS

Having to thank everyone else who helped make this book possible makes me appreciate the difficulty of winning an Academy Award. Except that I'm not eating up valuable TV time and you can read this at your leisure. If at all.

Anyway, I'll start with Anne Stockwell, Bruce Steele, and Judy Wieder at *The Advocate*, who supported this harebrained scheme of mine from the get-go and helped to make it all happen. The folks at Alyson Books—particularly Angela Brown, Danielle McCole, Tiffany Watson, Dan Cullinane, Whitney Friedlander, and Amy Martin (my comics pusher)—made this thing look and read much better than it had any right to. Special thanks to Corey Eubanks, Marcus Hu, Jack Plotnick, Lewis Tice, and everyone else who provided images.

I wouldn't be forming sentences without the molding of every English and journalism teacher I ever had, especially Peggy Dyer McNash, Pat Nunnally, Bobbi Alford, and Cleo Hudson. The latter's pronouncements on the sparing use of "to be" still reverberate through my brain whenever I write. And while I met only one of them, and for a very brief moment, I wouldn't be writing this book without the inspiration of Vito Russo, Pauline Kael, and Danny Peary. The late Ed Margulies and the extraordinary Stephen Rebello, in addition to being amazing dudes, have been far more influential than I'm sure they know. Also playing a key role in shaping my lifelong film obsession were my late parents as well as my siblings: Maria, Yoli, Xavier, Rod, and Chiky, thanks for letting me stay up for all those late shows and for driving me to all those movies. Appreciation with extra butter to Fernando for coming home from Harvard with all those books about Greta Garbo and the golden age of Hollywood. And thanks again for taking me to see *Diva* and *The North Avenue Irregulars*.

My friends have all been amazing throughout this entire process. For willingly being my focus group, mad props to Robert Abele, Sean Abley, Christopher Harrity, Dennis Hensley, Bob(aloo) Koenig, Mary Jo Pehl, Stephen Rebello, Kevin Sonnichsen, Tony Tripoli, and Donovan Whitehurst. Thanks also to Aaron Aldorisio, Ann Alexander, LD Beghtol, Suzanne Bridgeman, John Carrozza, Craig Chester, Katherine Connella, Gary Cotti, Charlotte Del Rose, Jerry Douglas, Michele Fleury, Tom Ford, Bryan Fuller, Michael Hastings, Curt Holman, Steve Holyer, Laura Kim, Kim Koster, Vincent Lopez, Terence McFarland, Christian McLaughlin, Ana Mullen, Joey O'Bryan, Jill Oliver, Jenni Olson, Clark Parsons, Doug Prinzivalli, Erin Quill, Loretta Ramos, Margy Rochlin, Mark Salzberg, Matt Zoller Seitz, Dennis Smeal, Kate Smeal, Curtis Tsui, John Waters, David Zeve, and Dave Cobb and Jason Havard and the Tuesday night dinner group for constantly being a source of inspiration. I also appreciate the input and insight of the hard-working staff of 20/20 Video in West Hollywood, Calif.

Finally, and hardly least, the big love to Dave White, without whom I would be a mere shell (with glasses). Without your input, your patience, and your occasional hectoring, there would be no book.

INTRODUCTION

OK, so maybe *must* is too strong a word. Maybe not. In any event, I felt compelled, as a lifelong film nerd, to create this list.

Let me give you a little backstory first: I'm told that when I learned to read, the first application of this new skill was devoted to reading the movie page of the newspaper, and soon I could tell you what was showing at any theater within a 10-mile radius of our house. (For some reason, I have a clear memory of the Russ Meyer title *Finders Keepers, Lovers Weepers!* (1968), but that's neither here nor there.) At the age of 4, my sister and one of her high school suitors took me to see *Willy Wonka & the Chocolate Factory* (1971), which probably warped my perceptions for life. By the time I was 11, I was begging my mom to drive me across town to one of Atlanta's two repertory theaters so I could finally see *Citizen Kane* (1941). I still remember watching *Making Love* (1982) on cable and holding my breath in the hope that my mother wouldn't notice I was in the room. To this day, I have a hard time remembering the names of friends and family members, but I have a ridiculous skill for calling up the résumés of character actors past and present. Like I said—nerd.

Why this book? I attribute it to a series of eager, well-scrubbed collegiate interns who've worked here at *The Advocate* over the years. They're great guys and gals, but I was flabbergasted at how many of these 20-somethings had seemingly no knowledge of any movie made before, oh, *The Matrix*. And while I've never seen myself as one of those queens who scowls into his brandy Alexander at these kids who've never heard of Lupe Velez, I was knocked for a loop to discover otherwise bright young adults who had somehow gotten this far in life without someone to sit them down and show them *Female Trouble* (1974) and *The Living End* (1992) and *Sunday Bloody Sunday* (1971) and *Go Fish* (1994). I was a few months into writing what I hoped would be a fun and informative movie guide when three gay friends around my own age mentioned to me that they were about to watch *All About Eve* (1950) for the first time, and I suddenly felt very justified at taking on this project.

Let me be clear about one thing right away—I don't for a second believe in any blanket statements that indicate that "All gay men love this" or "All gay men hate that." We're a crazily diverse bunch, politically, aesthetically, you name it. There are gay men who vote Republican. There are gay men who have mullets. Any group you can think of—Muslims, computer programmers, NASCAR fans, the homeless, Virgos, bowlers—has a subset of gay men. Gay men drink Pabst Blue Ribbon. Gay men read *Cat Fancy*. Gay men are Navy SEALs. So if I think the movies in this book are of gay interest, I'm working from a few assumptions that may or may not be true:

GAY MEN ADMIRE STRONG WOMEN. I'm not saying that gay men act like women or want to be women, necessarily, but I think we appreciate a woman with a backbone. In the same way that the world wants to treat all fags like effeminate puffballs with a talent for window treatments, women have had to endure a history of being pushed back into the kitchen. We respect them for standing up for themselves. And we know what a drag it is to have to be in romantic relationships with men. So gay guys (I think) are down, in general, with the ladies and their struggles.

GAY MEN LIKE WATCHING STRONG WOMEN FALL ON THEIR FACE. This might seem cruel, but it's almost a necessary corollary to the earlier assertion. Straight men tend to bury their emotions, so it's rare to watch a man in the movies hoist himself on the petard of his monstrous ego. (Sure, there's Kevin Costner's *The Postman* (1997), but what fun is *that* shitheap to watch?) When Diana Ross or Faye Dunaway or Mariah Carey dream big and fail, they fail big. And I want to be in the front row.

GAY MEN SEE THROUGH THE LIE THAT IS 99% OF ALL ART. As Harvey Fierstein once observed, practically every movie, book, TV show, and billboard we see throughout our lives tells us that we're supposed to marry a physically appealing woman, buy a house in the suburbs, and crank out the kids. And not that there's anything wrong with that, but it's this kind of propaganda that sets off a lot of homo bullshit detectors. As queer writer-director Alan Ball once told *Time* magazine, growing up gay means "you have a pretty deeply ingrained sense of being an outsider. You don't swallow the mythology of pop culture hook, line, and sinker because you know it's not true, for you, anyway."

GAY MEN KNOW WHAT IT'S LIKE TO BE LEFT OUTSIDE OF THE BIG TENT. I don't want to get into the whole my-minority-was-more-oppressed-than-your-minority argument with women or African Americans or anyone else, because it's beside the point. If you're a gay man in contemporary society, you know the feeling of exclusion, whether it's because your parents kicked you out of the house or some religious asshole got in your face at a pride parade or even just because some bigot gave you the fish-eye when you kissed your boyfriend at the airport.

Your queer mileage, as mentioned, may vary. But ultimately, this list is completely subjective, so don't be surprised if you're appalled by any of my inclusions or exclusions. If you're miffed that I left out *The Wizard of Oz* (1939) or *Those Who Love Me Can Take the Train* (1998) or *Steel Magnolias* (1989), well, deal with it. Or what the heck, write your own book. But before you do, I thank you for reading this one. And if you have any suggestions for *BRIDE OF 101 MUST-SEE MOVIES FOR GAY MEN* (knock wood), feel free to send them along to me at 101GayMovies@AdvocateBooks.com.

GUIDE TO SYMBOLS

 Art Directed as All-Get-Out: Films where the aesthetic is "more is more." Elaborate sets, camera movements, costumes, and editing that leap off the screen and smack you upside the head.

Aa **Art With a Capital A:** Or Cinema with a Capital C. These are movies that inspire doctoral theses and not drinking games.

 Bad Old Days: A reminder of how crappy queer lives were back in the day, before queer film festivals, the overturning of the sodomy law, and gay cable channels.

 Beautiful Disaster: Those delicious cinematic car accidents from which you can't divert your eyes. In fact, you'll likely circle around the block and drive by again for a closer look.

 Closet Be Damned: Movies that include coming out, even if they aren't specifically coming-out movies.

Divas on the Rampage: Larger-than-life personalities shoving everyone around, taking center stage, and stealing focus. And divas don't have to be female.

Fuck Shit Up: All bets are off. These are movies that are as unpredictable, raucous, and in-your-face as great punk rock.

 Funny Uncle: Movies that are favorites of the pre-Stonewall generation that remain entertaining to this day.

 Gays With Guns: No, that is a pistol in their pocket, and they may or may not be happy to see you.

 Genderfucky: Boys who dress like girls. Women who act like men. Dudes who are between surgeries. It's all in here.

 Get Out Your Handkerchiefs: Movies that are happy or sad, but guaranteed to make you cry, unless you're some sort of heartless bastard.

 Man-on-Man Action: Could be kissing, could be the horizontal mambo, but the guys are getting *something*.

 Muh-YOOsical!: Show tunes, disco, tap dancing, you name it. And don't act like you're too cool for a good number.

+/- **Negative? Positive? You Decide:** Movies that still cause arguments in the gay community. Plan time for a little post-screening discussion if necessary.

 1980 Is 1979 Plus Nothing: One of the trickier turn-of-the-decades for filmmakers to pull off without total embarrassment. (And yes, I know that technically, the '70s lasted from 1971 to 1980. Shut up.)

Snuggle on the Sofa: Great date movies. If you aren't getting laid after (or during), you're just not trying hard enough.

Women Sexy Enough to Give Fags a Tingle: Just because we don't necessarily want to sleep with them, it doesn't mean we can't appreciate a foxy lady.

Words to Live By: Movies you'll quote voraciously until your dearest friends are forced to stage an intervention.

Would It Kill You to Watch a Lesbian Movie?: Seriously. Give it up to the sisters. These are cool movies about how the other half of the queer nation lives.

101
MUST-SEE
MOVIES
FOR
GAY MEN

ALL ABOUT EVE

(1950)

Written and directed by Joseph L. Mankiewicz.
Bette Davis, Anne Baxter, Celeste Holm, George Sanders,
Gary Merrill, Hugh Marlowe, Marilyn Monroe.
(Twentieth Century Fox Home Entertainment)

Broadway star Margo Channing (Davis) is an icon of the stage and in love with director Bill Sampson (Merrill). But the fact that she's just turned 40 nags at her, and it makes her vulnerable to a serpent in the garden: Eve (Baxter). Mousy little Eve seems nice as pie at first, eager to please and help out Margo, whom she worships. But soon it becomes clear to Margo, Bill, and Margo's best friend, Karen (Holm), that Eve is a little minx not to be trusted. Not that her deviousness will stop her from being Broadway's *next* big star.

★ ★

OK, this book is an alphabetical listing, but I probably would have put *All About Eve* at or near the top anyway. A deliciously overwritten and wittily pungent story about Broadway backstabbers, this movie practically created the "drama queen." From Davis's wonderfully star-sized performance to George Sanders's viperish theater columnist Addison DeWitt to Marilyn

Monroe's small role as a sexy young ingenue, the cast chews up and spits out Mankiewicz's richly verbose script to perfection. While it seems like *All About Eve* is ingrained in every gay man's DNA, I was shocked to discover how many friends of mine had made it well into their 30s without having seen it. And so, this book.

Quotes to Remember:

As iconic as it is, leave "Fasten your seat belts, it's going to be a bumpy night" to the amateurs and the staff writers at *Will & Grace*. There are plenty of other gems to be uncovered from *Eve*, including:

> **Margo:** I'm not to be had for the price of a cocktail...like a salted peanut.

> **Margo** (angrily, to Eve): And stop treating me like I was the Queen Mother!
> **Bill:** Outside of a beehive, Margo, your behavior tonight would qualify as neither queenly nor motherly.

> **Karen** (upon hearing Margo plans to get married): What will you wear?
> **Margo:** Something simple. A mink coat over a nightgown.

Advanced viewers of *All About Eve* can get laughs from each other with such fleeting sentiments as "I call myself Phoebe" and "Fire and music! Some sparklers and a kazoo." But please, wait until after at least three viewings before you attempt them.

ALL ABOUT MY MOTHER

(1999)

Written and directed by Pedro Almodóvar.
Cecilia Roth, Marisa Paredes, Candela Peña, Antonia San Juan,
Penélope Cruz. (Sony Pictures Home Entertainment)

Nurse Manuela (Roth) takes her son to a Madrid production of *A Streetcar Named Desire* on his 18th birthday. Afterward, he is struck by a car and killed while trying to pursue legendary actress Huma Rojo (Paredes) for an autograph. Grief-stricken, Manuela goes to Barcelona to find her son's father, who now sports an impressive pair of knockers and goes by the name "Lola." While she doesn't find Lola, Manuela does run into her transgender friend Agrado (San Juan), who in turn introduces her to friendly nun Rosa (Cruz). It turns out that Rosa is pregnant and HIV-positive—and once again, Lola is the father. Huma eventually becomes part of their circle as well, as the *Streetcar* troupe has come to Barcelona and Manuela gets a job as her assistant. Through deaths, births, and illness, these women provide each other with the strength that no man could.

★ ★

It was difficult to pick just one Almodóvar film for this book, as he is one of today's greatest filmmakers. But *All About My Mother* represents, I think, the most successful fruition of many of his themes and obsessions. It's a "women's picture"; an homage to backstage dramas like *All About Eve* (see p. 1) and John Cassavetes's *Opening Night* (1977); a meditation on love, sex, and gender; and a celebration of motherhood, and womanhood in general—almost all of the men in the movie that don't turn themselves into women either die or lose their minds. It's very funny at times; at others, it's gut-wrenchingly sad. See it with the people around you who you think of as family, biological or otherwise.

Fun facts:

★ Manuela's character—a nurse who helps teach doctors how to ask bereaved relatives to make organ donations from their dead loved ones—first surfaced in Almodóvar's *The Flower of My Secret* (1995).

★ Almodóvar likes to use the same actors again and again: Besides Roth and Paredes, longtime Almodóvar veterans, fans will notice that the doctor in the stage production of *Streetcar* played the duplicitous Iván in *Women on the Verge of a Nervous Breakdown* (1988) and that the recipient of Manuela's son's heart turns up as the bullfighter's brother-in-law in *Talk to Her* (2002).

★ There's a play on words in the Spanish title of the film that's not quite as vivid in English. At the beginning of the movie, Manuela and her son discuss the fact that *All About Eve* was given a slightly different title in Spanish because the literal translation, *Todo Sobre Eva*, sounds awkward. This is because

Cecilia Roth (Manuela) and Eloy Azorín (Manuela's son)

"sobre" means "about" but also "on top of" or "covering." So the Spanish title *Todo Sobre Mi Madre* means "all about my mother" but also "everything on top of my mother," in reference to the burdens Manuela must bear. (For that matter, the English title's "about" has more than one meaning.)

Quote to Remember:

Agrado: All I have that's real are my feelings and these pints of silicone that weigh a ton.

AUTEUR ALERT:

Go out and see everything Almodóvar ever made. His career has followed an interesting trajectory—his first film, *Pepi, Luci, Bom* (1980), earned him the reputation as the "Spanish John Waters" (see p. 5), but his career has followed a significantly different trajectory than the Pope of Trash's. My personal favorites: *Women on the Verge of a Nervous Breakdown, Law of Desire* (1987), *Talk to Her, Labyrinth of Passion* (1982), *Bad Education* (2004), *Matador* (1986), *What Have I Done to Deserve This?* (1984).

THE
APPLE

(1980)

**Written by Menahem Golan, from an idea by
Coby and Iris Recht. Directed by Menahem Golan.**
Catherine Mary Stewart, George Gilmour, Grace Kennedy, Alan Love,
Vladek Sheybal, Joss Ackland, Ray Shell. (MGM Home Entertainment)

T ry to follow this one: In the future world of 1994, rock
and roll is run by the BIM, or Boogalow International
Music. And running the BIM is the nefarious Mr.
Boogalow (Sheybal). He rigs the Worldvision Song
Contest to keep Canadian balladeers Alphie (Gilmour) and Bibi
(Stewart) from winning, but tries to sign them both up as
clients. Bibi happily joins him, but Alphie has a vision of Mr.
Boogalow as Satan leading the duo (as Adam and Eve) into
temptation. Bibi becomes a big star, but realizes she misses
Alphie. He rescues her and takes her to live with the hippies in
the park. A year later, the BIM comes after Bibi for breach of
contract, but then Mr. Topps (Ackland) parks his golden Rolls
Royce in the sky and comes down to take Alphie, Bibi, and all
the hippies to another world where they can escape Boogalow's
influence.

★ ★

Hoo boy—it's an awful musical *and* a ridiculous biblical
allegory, all rolled up into one! An utter disaster for the then-
fledgling Cannon Films in 1980—the company would go on to
make some of that decade's schlockiest and more profitable

movies, most of them starring Chuck Norris—*The Apple* became
a cult sensation after popping up at Los Angeles's NuArt
Theater in the 2003 midnight movie series. The songs are ludicrous (although admittedly catchy), and the choreography has to
be seen to be believed. But what's most fascinating about *The
Apple* is its vision of "the future." The movie is packed with fey
Euro-types, tons of cameltoe (male and female), ugly drag
queens with feather boas, and the prissiest backup dancers
deutschmarks could buy. But check out Boogalow's henchmen
Ashley and Mr. Shake—if fagginess was radioactive, these two
could power a cyclotron. Like *Can't Stop the Music* (see p. 43)
and *Xanadu* (see p. 240), *The Apple* is a 1980 movie that didn't
see the '80s coming. All three movies assumed that the coming
decade would be just like the 1970s, only more so; *The Apple*
foresees a 1994 where the dominant fashion statement in music
isn't the flannel shirt—instead it's dramatic eye makeup and
beard glitter and shimmering jumpsuits with giant shoulders.
Perhaps it's a pity that this particular vision didn't come true.

Fun Facts:

★ Legend has it that opening-day patrons of *The Apple* in Los
Angeles were given free copies of the soundtrack album on
the way into the theater and that these viewers were so
incensed by the film that they pelted said records at the
screen. Theater managers tried giving the albums to audiences
on their way out of subsequent screenings only to discover
that, after seeing the movie, no one wanted to ever hear those
songs again. Ironically, those same soundtrack albums now
fetch a pretty penny on eBay.

★ That's soap star and *Staying Alive* (1983) diva Finola Hughes as
one of the backup dancers; she gets a big fat close-up in the
unforgettable "Speed" (or should I say, "Sp-e-e-e-d!") number.

★ Does the single-entendre sex ballad "Coming for You" sound familiar? Dig out a Donna Summer album track from a few years before *The Apple* called "Wasted." If Giorgio Moroder felt litigious about it, there's not a jury on Earth that wouldn't take his side.

AUNTIE MAME

(1958)

Written by Betty Comden and Adolph Green,
based on the play by Jerome Lawrence and Robert E. Lee,
based on the novel by Patrick Dennis.
Directed by Morton daCosta.
Rosalind Russell, Forrest Tucker, Coral Browne, Fred Clark, Peggy
Cass, Joanna Barnes. (Warner Bros. Home Video)

Manhattan socialite Mame Dennis (Russell) finds herself taking care of her young nephew Patrick after the death of her brother. Armed with her motto—"Life is a banquet, and most poor suckers are starving to death"—she strives to open the boy's mind to all possibilities. Doing his best to pigeonhole Patrick into a conservative and conformist upbringing is his father's executor, Dwight Babcock (Clark). Mame marries and loses rich Southern gentleman Beau (Tucker), writes her memoirs, and saves Patrick from marrying "Aryan from Darien" Gloria Upson (Barnes).

★ ★

Countless kids in countless suburbs saw this movie on TV and dreamed of being whisked away to New York City to live with an outsized eccentric like Auntie Mame. Heaven knows I did. Russell brings this wonderful character to very vivid life, and her zeal for living—not to mention those constant wardrobe and interior design changes—have made Mame a queer icon for the

ages. But while Russell is very much the star, she's ably supported by a cast of delicious character actors like Coral Browne (as
boozy Broadway star Vera Charles), Peggy Cass (clueless steno
Agnes Gooch), and Barnes, all of whom play women who would
make perfect Halloween costumes for men. (But please, can we
have a moratorium on gay men using "Life is a banquet" as a
motto in their online profiles? That shit is tired.)

Quotes to Remember:

> **Patrick:** What's that, Auntie Mame?
> **Mame:** It's a B, dear. The first in a seven-letter word meaning
> your late father.

> **Mame** (hungover in bed, after Patrick has abruptly drawn the
> shades): My dear! How can you see with all that light?

> **Gloria:** Oh, you'd love Montebank. It's awfully exclusive
> and terribly restricted.
> **Mame:** Exclusive to what and restricted to whom?

> **Agnes** (staggering in from her first wild evening out): I did
> exactly what she told me. I lived! Now I have to find out what I'm
> supposed to do next.

> **Vera** (being handed a copy of Mame's memoirs): I've been to so
> many wonderful parties here. Now I can find out how they all ended.

See Also:

Feeling masochistic? Check out the wretched Lucille Ball musical
Mame, which proved that, by 1974, the 63-year-old star was no
longer the chorine she once was. If nothing else, fast-forward to
watch all of Bea Arthur's scenes as Vera.

BARBARELLA

(1968)

**Written by Terry Southern and Roger Vadim &
Vittorio Bonicelli & Clement Biddle Wood &
Brian Degas & Tudor Gates & Jean-Claude Forest**,
based on the comic book by Jean-Claude Forest and Claude Brulé.
Directed by Roger Vadim.
Jane Fonda, John Phillip Law, Anita Pallenberg, Milo O'Shea, Marcel
Marceau, David Hemmings, Ugo Tognazzi.
(Paramount Home Entertainment)

S exy astronavigatrix Barbarella (Fonda) is the only hope for the pacified Earth of the future when rogue scientist Durand Durand disappears into an uncharted patch of the universe with the plans for a sinister weapon. She is helped on her mission by a child-catcher (Tognazzi), a blind angel (Law), and a befuddled revolutionary (Hemmings); she repays them all with sex after learning how to make love "the old-fashioned way." Eventually, Barbarella tracks down Durand Durand, but before he can commence a reign of terror, the entire city of Sogo is swallowed up by the Mathmos, a living liquid that feeds on evil.

★ ★

OK, any movie that inspires two band names—'80s faves Duran Duran and experimental electronic combo Matmos—automatically has stature as a pop culture touchstone. But *Barbarella* is silly, sexy, and entertaining on all fronts. Fonda plays the character as something of a wide-eyed ingenue, but

John Philip Law (Pygar) and Jane Fonda (Barbarella)

even though director Vadim (Fonda's husband at the time) dresses her in a series of fetishistic outfits—using crazy combinations of plastic, fur, leather, chain mail, you name it—you never feel like she's being exploited. Barbarella is in control and, importantly, getting off on the sex. (And if the future isn't about awesome sex, what's the point of living?) Opponents of Jane Fonda's stances on the Vietnam war and feminism have tried to hold this movie against her, but she's always had a sense of humor about it; now that Fonda is long past her moment in the political spotlight, audiences can still enjoy the low-tech special effects (including Fonda's legendary zero-gravity striptease), the deadpan dialogue ("This is really much too poetic a way to die," says Barbarella, as tiny birds nip at her), and the general atmosphere of goofy eroticism. Add the utterly ludicrous theme song

("Barbarella psychedella / There's a kind of cockleshell about you"), and you've got a perfectly dopey way to spend an evening.

See Also:

Producer Dino De Laurentiis recycled some of the sets (and cast) from this film into Mario Bava's kooky cat-burglar epic *Danger: Diabolik* (1968). It's a supremely silly piece of Eurotrash—and was, in fact, featured on the very last episode of that great show about bad movies, *Mystery Science Theater 3000*—but such delicious eye candy that director Roman Coppola visually quotes it throughout his tribute to '60s cinema, *CQ* (2001). Joseph Losey's 1966 *Modesty Blaise* also features a secret-agent sex kitten (Monica Vitti) in a series of outrageous pop-art sets and costumes.

BASIC INSTINCT

(1992)

Written by Joe Eszterhas.
Directed by Paul Verhoeven.
Michael Douglas, Sharon Stone, Jeanne Tripplehorn, George Dzundza,
Leilani Sarelle, Dorothy Malone. (Artisan Home Video)

The prime suspect in the brutal ice-pick stabbing of a former rock star is novelist Catherine Trammell (Stone), at least partially because she had written a book two years prior about a woman who stabs a former rock star to death with an ice pick. The police, notably Detective Nick Curran (Douglas), try to pin the murder on her, but she's too cool a customer for them. Soon, the bodies start piling up, and the murders all look like Catherine did them and tried to make them look like the work of Nick, who she's started sleeping with as research for her new novel, about an out-of-control police detective. But she's not the only suspect: What about bisexual Catherine's soft butch girlfriend, Roxy (Sarelle)? Or police psychiatrist Beth (Tripplehorn), who's having an affair with Nick but has ties to Catherine from her college days? It's all wrapped up in an exposition-heavy finish, but the resolution to the mystery makes about as much sense as the three arbitrary endings to *Clue* (1985).

★ ★

Basic Instinct single-handedly kicked off a post-ACT UP wave of queer activism, as gays and lesbians targeted this film as an example of how the very few screen representations of homosexuals tended to be negative ones. After all the hue and cry, the movie wound up being a gigantic hit anyway (giving Verhoeven and Eszterhas the clout to make *Showgirls*—see p. 180). But something else happened as well—more than a few lesbians discovered that there were worse things than having a bisexual murder suspect played by sexy Sharon Stone. The character of Catherine shrewdly manipulates everything that's going on around her—"She's evil! She's brilliant!" shouts Beth at one point, hilariously—and wound up becoming something of a riot-grrrl-in-couture icon. Sort of like the cartoon character Hothead Paisan: Homicidal Lesbian Terrorist, only with better hair. (And yes, you do get to see her bush.)

Quotes to Remember:

> **Nick** (to Roxy): "Let me ask you something, *Rocky*—man to man—I think she's the fuck of the century. What do you think?"

> **Beth:** "What was I supposed to say? 'Hey guys, I'm not gay, but I fucked your suspect'?"

 +/-

BEAR CUB

(2004)

Written by Miguel Albaladejo and Salvador García Ruiz.
Directed by Miguel Albaladejo.
José Luis García Pérez, David Castillo, Empar Ferer, Elvira Lindo, Arno Chevrier. (TLA Home Video)

P edro (García Pérez) is a gay Madrid dentist who's stocky and bearded—a "bear," in gay parlance. His flaky sister dashes off to India for a month, leaving her 9-year-old son Bernardo (Castillo) in his care. She gets arrested on a narcotics charge, and the sex-and-drugs-loving Pedro suddenly finds himself having to be a parent. Enter Doña Teresa (Ferer), Bernardo's paternal grandmother, whom Bernardo's mom has always aggressively kept out of the picture. She wants to get close to the child and will resort to any means to elbow her way into his life. Will the newly paternal Pedro get to keep his charge?

★ ★

While *Bear Cub* falls alongside movies like *Central Station* (1998), *Kolya* (1996), and *Baby Boom* (1987)—adorable child melts heart of gruff loner—it's smart enough not to feel like a collection of clichés. For one thing, it's a gay movie full of beard-ed dudes who eat carbs, which feels practically controversial when compared to the rest of gay cinema. (True story: I attended a press conference for a short-lived TV show called *Normal, Ohio*, which starred the husky John Goodman as a gay dad. A woman sitting in front of me asked the actor if he was going to

David Castillo (Bernardo) and José Luis García Pérez (Pedro)

lose weight so that he could play a gay guy. She later told me that her only impression of gay men were the specimens walking in and out of the Crunch gym in West Hollywood. I responded by flashing my gut at her.) The novelty of beardom aside, however, it's the delicious performances by García Pérez and Castillo that really make the movie take off. Even if the notion of parenting carries no sentimental weight for you at all, you'll enjoy watching these two disparate personalities create a family between them.

BEAUTIFUL THING

(1996)

Written by Jonathan Harvey, based on his play.
Directed by Hettie MacDonald.
Glen Berry, Scott Neal, Linda Henry, Tameka Empson.
(Sony Pictures Home Entertainment)

Teenage Jamie (Berry) lives with his mother, Sandra (Henry), in Thamesmead, one of those soul-draining rat's mazes of a modern housing development. The two bicker incessantly but have a fairly loving relationship. The same cannot be said for Ste (Neal), who lives next door with his abusive father and brother. Ste takes refuge at Sandra's and winds up sharing a bed with Jamie. The two discover they have feelings for each other, although popular athlete Ste can't immediately face up to it. Sandra eventually realizes what's going on, as does Mama Cass–obsessed neighbor Leah (Empson).

★ ★

While *Beautiful Thing* belongs firmly in the kitchen sink-Mike Leigh school of working-class British naturalism, its sweet gay love story about two adorable teens who find solace in each other's arms makes audiences go all swoony. The film features people treating each other horribly, young adults facing bleak futures, and a handful of really unfortunate hairdos, but you'll leave the movie with a big, dumb grin on your face. Who can resist a soundtrack full of yearning love songs from Mama Cass and a seduction scene scored to "Sixteen Going on Seventeen"? It will be interesting to see how this film ages—after all, today's teens are growing up in a world of gay-straight alliances and same-sex prom dates. After enough time, *Beautiful Thing* may be thought of as a relic from the age when it was unusual to be out and in a relationship while still in high school.

Quotes to Remember:

Ste: Do you think I'm queer?
Jamie: It don't matter what I think.

Sandra: There's me going to bed of a night worried 'cause you had to share a bed with Ste, and all this time you were doing the 70 minus one. I like the lad, Jamie, but he hasn't seen any life.
Jamie: But he's good to me.
Sandra: Is he?
Jamie: Yeah.

Sandra: You think I want these flats infamous for child murder? No, I won't be telling your dad.
Ste (near tears): He'd kill me.
Sandra: Yeah, I just said that.
Ste: No, he would.
Sandra: Yeah, I think we've established that, actually, Ste.
Ste: They all would.
Sandra: I'll bloody kill you in a minute if you don't stop sniveling and shut up. [Pause] Look, you're a good kid, and that's what counts. And somewhere, you'll find people that don't want to kill you.

Ste: Do you want to go to the Gloucester?
Leah: Do what?
Ste: Gay pub.
Leah: Don't know any gay blokes.

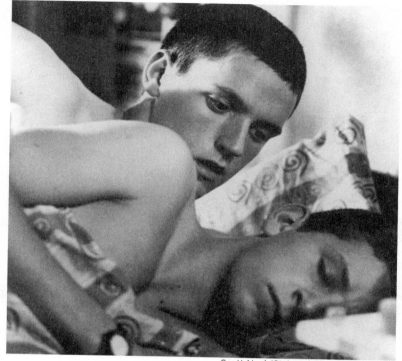

Scott Neal (Ste) and Glen Berry (Jamie)

Ste: Yes you do.

Leah: Yeah?

Ste: Yeah. There'll be plenty of men.

Leah: Yeah, and they'll all dance backwards and never get married.

Ste (reading from *Gay Times*): "You cannot transmit the HIV virus via frottage." What's frottage?

Jamie: It's yogurt. It's French.

See Also:

David Moreton's sweet coming-of-age tale *Edge of Seventeen* (1998), probably the closest an American film has come to capturing young queer love. The somewhat erratic British dramedy *Get Real* (1998) also merits a look. And finally, there's the Sid and Marty Krofft extravaganza *Pufnstuf* (1970), which features another great stealth gay anthem from Mama Cass, "Different is Hard."

BEYOND THE VALLEY OF THE DOLLS

(1970)

Written by Roger Ebert,
based on a story by Roger Ebert and Russ Meyer.
Directed by Russ Meyer.
Dolly Read, Cynthia Myers, Marcia McBroom, John Lazar,
Michael Blodgett, Edy Williams, Erica Gavin, David Gurian.
(Twentieth Century Fox Home Entertainment)

Singers Kelly (Read), Casey (Myers), and Petronella (McBroom) take their rock combo, the Kelly Affair, to Los Angeles under the guidance of their manager (and Kelly's lover) Harris (Gurian). The group soon falls under the tutelage of super-producer Ronnie "Z-Man" Barzell (Lazar), who renames them the Carrie Nations. Kelly finds herself torn between Harris and gigolo Lance Rocke (Blodgett), Pet cheats on her nice-guy law student boyfriend with a pro football player, and Casey falls in love with a lesbian fashion designer (Gavin). After much tragedy—including a drug-fueled orgy in which Lance, Casey, and her lover are murdered by turns-out-he's-a-woman Z-Man—there's a happy ending of sorts.

★ ★

In no real way a sequel to the original *Valley of the Dolls* (p.

216)—Jacqueline Susann's estate sued Twentieth Century Fox and won, claiming that this similarly-titled X-rated morality play demeaned the author's original work—*BVD* is nonsensical, hallucinatory, and ridiculous. Whether or not director Russ Meyer and writer Roger Ebert—yes, *that* Roger Ebert—intended it to be so remains up for interpretation. While it doesn't have the crackle of Meyer's black and white go-go masterpiece *Faster, Pussycat! Kill! Kill!* (1965), there's still a palpable sense of excitement to *BVD*. The songs are catchy, the girls are stacked, and big chunks of it remain puzzling and bizarre even after repeated viewings. I remain annoyed by the lesbian-fellates-gun sequence—and by the fact that Meyer and Ebert kill the lesbians (who haven't treated anyone badly), the bi guy, and the tranny, but give everyone else a cheery denouement—but I keep coming back to *BVD* because it's just bananas. In the best way.

Quotes to Remember:

Z-Man: This is my happening, and it freaks me out!

Porn star Ashley St. Ives (Williams): You're a groovy boy. I'd like to strap you on sometime.

BIG EDEN

(2000)

Written and directed by Thomas Bezucha.
Arye Gross, Eric Schweig, Tim DeKay, Louise Fletcher,
George Coe, Veanne Cox, Nan Martin. (Wolfe Video)

On the eve of his first big gallery show in New York, Henry (Gross) is called back to his hometown in Montana after his grandfather Sam (Coe) suffers a stroke. Henry's never told Sam that he's gay—although it's pretty clear that Sam knows already—which makes it all the more complicated when Henry realizes his old best friend-slash-crush from high school, Dean (DeKay), is also back in town. Unbeknownst to Henry, another old high school chum is carrying a torch for him—reticent Native American Pike (Schweig), who runs the general store. The whole town of loving busybodies observes the Henry-Dean-Pike triangle, but Henry remains oblivious. Will he find true love? Or will he leave behind a small town that adores him to return to the bright lights of Manhattan?

★ ★

Let's talk for a minute about what *Big Eden* isn't: It isn't about an urban gay man and his bitchy friends. It doesn't have any house music or anyone doing drag. It's not about gay men who look like hunky, buff porn stars. It doesn't say that gay people have to run away from their dysfunctional families and their

Arye Gross (Henry) and Eric Schweig (Pike)

stifling small towns to find fulfillment as adults. Not that there's
necessarily anything wrong with those things, but they became
clichés in the films that followed the bold New Queer Cinema
titles of the early 1990s. If only for avoiding these pitfalls, *Big
Eden* would be a breath of fresh air among queer cinema, but it's
more than just the anti-*Broken Hearts Club*. (see p. 34) It's a
wonderfully written romantic comedy with poignant moments
that are never sappy, set in one of those magical small-town fan-
tasylands where everyone's all up in each other's business, but
always in a sweet, well-intentioned, and completely nonhomo-
phobic way. *Big Eden*'s utopian vision is a cinematic response to
the famous Gandhi saying about becoming the change you wish
to see in the world. And despite the fact that it was made on a
medium-sized budget, it's got a great cast and beautiful cinematography. (The fact that it's shot among the breathtaking
lakes and mountains of Montana certainly doesn't hurt.) *Big
Eden* is a little miracle. And it's the kind of gay film you could
actually watch with your parents.

Quotes to Remember:

Mary-Margaret (to Henry): Maybe this means you can finally tell Sam you're gay, put some of that therapy to use. He knows, you know, I don't have to tell you that. You don't imagine he hasn't figured out there might be a reasonable explanation for the fact that the last time you had a girlfriend you were also in the third grade?

Jim, a townie (to Pike): There's so few nice surprises in life. Seems to me it's kind of a shame to squander one of them, don't you think?

BOOM!

(1968)

Written by Tennessee Williams,
based on his play *The Milk Train Doesn't Stop Here Anymore*.
Directed by Joseph Losey.
Elizabeth Taylor, Richard Burton, Noel Coward,
Joanna Shimkus, Michael Dunn. (VHS only; Universal Home Video)

Sissy Goforth (Taylor, too young for the role) is the world's richest woman, having outlived six husbands. Now she lays dying in her island fortress off the coast of Sardinia. Not coincidentally, her imminent demise draws in mendicant poet Chris Flanders (Burton, too old for the role), known for his ability to woo rich women on their deathbeds. Sissy cries for "Injections!" and narrates her memoirs to her long-suffering assistant Blackie (Shimkus) while Chris wanders about the estate. Fortune-teller "the Witch of Capri" (Coward) drops by for a lunch of "boiled sea monster" and gets drunk. Sissy and Chris yell at each other and drink. Finally, *finally*, Sissy drops dead.

★ ★

The combo of Elizabeth Taylor and Tennessee Williams reached the heights of *Cat on a Hot Tin Roof* (1958) and the middles of *Suddenly, Last Summer* (see p. 195) before plunging into magma with *Boom!*, one of many big-budget duds that Taylor & Burton Inc. cranked out before their divorces. Watching Boom! one imagines Mike Nichols realizing just how out-of-control his stars of *Who's Afraid of Virginia Woolf?* (1966) would have been without proper supervision. But, as John Waters has famously noted, *Boom!* is "failed art" and thus "perfect." As crazy scenery-chewing performances go, Taylor's here is one for the ages. (It's rumored that the Burtons and director Joseph Losey started every shooting day with a round of Bloody Marys. That explains why the couple wanted to buy the movie's house location, despite the fact that it was a set with *no roof*.) No wonder Waters has had something of a sideline career screening this madcap movie at festivals from Dallas to Locarno, Switzerland. Write Universal and beg them to release a letterboxed DVD version with a Waters commentary. It's the least they can do for a movie this extravagantly whacked-out.

Quotes to Remember:

Sissy: (to a clumsy servant): Shit on your mother!

The Witch of Capri: My heart beats blood that is not my blood, but the blood of anonymous blood donors.

Chris: In Xanadu did Kubla Khan a stately pleasure dome decree / Where Alph, the sacred river, ran through caverns measureless to man / Down to a sunless sea.
Sissy: *Wh-a-a-a-t?*

BOUND

(1996)

Written and directed by Andy Wachowski and Larry Wachowski.
Gina Gershon, Jennifer Tilly, Joe Pantoliano,
Chris Meloni. (Republic Home Video)

Newly sprung ex-con Corky (Gershon) gets a job refurbishing the apartment next door to mobster Caesar (Pantoliano) and his girlfriend, Violet (Tilly). Violet flirts with tough, tattooed Corky until the two finally start getting up close and personal. In the midst of all the heavy breathing, Caesar winds up in custody of $2 million in mob money. Violet convinces Corky to steal the money so the two of them can run away together. Is Violet playing Corky for a sap? Will Caesar figure out their scheme in time?

★ ★

This neo-noir classic, the movie the Wachowski siblings (one of the brothers may have become a sister by the time you read this) made before the *Matrix* trilogy, combines a wonderfully labyrinthine con game with some of the most breathlessly sexy girl-on-girl scenes ever featured in a mainstream movie. The Wachowskis wisely hired sapphic sexpert Susie Bright as a "technical advisor" to the film, so the Violet-Corky couplings don't play out as a straight guy's fantasy of what it is that gals do in bed together. (Although some lesbians may question the ladies' long fingernails in proximity to some sensitive areas.) The directors are clearly having fun contrasting femme Violet (who wears lingerie and tight dresses) and butch Corky (leather jackets and tighty-whities), but neither character plays like a two-dimensional stereotype. *Bound* is funny, suspenseful, and erotic—and I can't tell you how many gay men I know say, "I could never have sex with a woman. Except Gina Gershon."

Quotes to Remember:

Violet: You seem uncomfortable. Do I make you nervous, Corky?
Corky: No. [*Sips beer*]
Violet: Thirsty, maybe.
Corky: Curious, maybe.
Violet: That's funny. I'm feeling a little bit curious myself.

Corky: We're different.
Violet: We're not that different, Corky.
Corky: Ah, let's see. This is the part where you tell me what matters is on the inside, and that inside of you there's a little dyke like me.
Violet: No, she's nothing like you. She's a whole lot smarter than you are.
Corky: Is that what her daddy tells her?
Violet: I know what I am. I don't have to have it tattooed on my shoulder.
Corky: You saying you don't have sex with men?
Violet: I don't.
Corky: (scoffs): For Christ's sake, Violet, I heard you. Thin walls, remember?
Violet: What you heard wasn't sex.
Corky: What the fuck was it?
Violet: Work. You made certain choices in your life that you paid for. You said you made them because you were good at something, and it was easy. You think you're the only person that's good at something? We make our own choices. We pay our own prices. I think we're more alike than you care to admit.

THE BOYS IN THE BAND

(1970)

Written by Mart Crowley,
based on his play.
Directed by William Friedkin.
Kenneth Nelson, Peter White, Leonard Frey, Cliff Gorman, Frederick
Combs, Laurence Luckinbill, Keith Prentice, Robert La Tourneaux,
Reuben Greene.
(VHS only. Not yet available on DVD—complain to Twentieth Century
Fox Home Entertainment)

A group of neurotic and painfully unhappy Stonewall-era gay men gather at a Manhattan apartment for a birthday party. An old college friend of the host—whom the host has long suspected of being a closet case—drops by, upset. Vicious party games are played, and devastating revelations are made.

★ ★

Oh, what can one say about *The Boys in the Band*? On the one hand, it's a somewhat embarrassing time capsule featuring a bunch of messed-up queens. On the other hand, the movie is riddled with hilarious and bitchy dialogue that at its best is as zingy as anything in *All About Eve* (p. 1). William Friedkin's direction—this flaming hetero also made *Cruising* (p. 58), go fig-ure—won't make you forget that this property started out stage-bound, but at least he keeps the pace brisk. And historically speaking, *Boys* will always be an important play and film in terms of being one of the first to treat gay characters like actual human beings. Even if modern audiences flinch at the self-hat-ing homos in *Boys*, the film remains a potent reminder that we have indeed come a long way, baby.

Quotes to Remember:

Tons, but it's hard to do any of them justice out of context. But here's a taste:

Michael: If we could just learn not to hate ourselves so much. That's it, you know. If we could just *learn* not to hate ourselves quite so very much.

See Also:

The Boys in the Band spawned a low-budget knockoff, *Some of My Best Friends Are* (1971), about a bunch of tragic queers spending Christmas Eve in a gay bar. The crackpot cast includes future TV stars Gil Gerard (of *Buck Rogers* fame, as a hunky pilot), Gary Sandy (playing a vicious hustler years before tuning in to *WKRP in Cincinnati*), Fannie Flagg (the *Match Game* panelist and future *Fried Green Tomatoes* author has a supporting role as hatcheck girl Mildred Pierce), and Rue McClanahan (as an evil fag hag). This movie once offended gay activists, but time has made it flat-out hilarious. If this unavailable-on-video gem—which turns up occasionally on Logo—ever screens anywhere near you, cancel all plans and go, go, go.

THE BROKEN HEARTS CLUB

(2000)

Written and directed by Greg Berlanti.
Timothy Olyphant, Dean Cain, Zach Braff, John Mahoney, Nia Long,
Mary McCormack, Matt McGrath, Justin Theroux, Jennifer Coolidge.
(Sony Pictures Home Entertainment)

A toxic group of West Hollywood gay men undermine their own and each other's relationships and grouse about their lot in life, two activities interrupted only by their occasional declarations about how much they love their friends and how they couldn't survive without them. The film's narrator (Olyphant) demonstrates how valuable these jerks are by fleeing them all to go to Europe at the end of the movie so he can get a life.

★ ★

I lied. This isn't a must-see—it's a must to avoid. I include *The Broken Hearts Club* here as an example of the truckload of crappy gay movies that have been produced since the early '90s. There was a time when it took writer-director Donna Deitch years and years to get enough money scraped together to make the exquisite *Desert Hearts* (1985), a groundbreaking lesbian love story. Now, film festivals are choked with hideous gay and lesbian features offering tissue-thin characterizations, sitcom plotting, glib sentimentality, and enough eye candy to make a marketable video box. *Club* isn't necessarily the worst of these movies—I would hate to think someone is sitting through all of them to have to make such a distinction—but it's one of the more high-profile ones. I suppose fags love it because it features famous hunks like Cain and Olyphant (and the not-yet-famous Braff) gaying it up, but I find *Club* to be like water torture, albeit with expensive designer mineral water. Remember: Just because it's gay doesn't mean it's good.

Also worth ducking:

Lie Down With Dogs (1995), *Friends and Family* (2001), *All Over the Guy* (2001), *Slutty Summer* (2005), *A Family Affair* (2001), *Jeffrey* (1995), *Everything Relative* (1996), *Men in Love* (1989), *Ordinary Sinner* (2001), and far too many more to mention.

BROTHER TO BROTHER (2004)

Written and directed by Rodney Evans.
Anthony Mackie, Duane Boutte, Daniel Sunjata, Roger Robinson, Aunjanue Ellis. (Wolfe Video)

P erry (Mackie) is a college student torn between two worlds—his fellow African-American classmates don't want to hear him discuss queer icons of literature, and the white guys he dates seem to fetishize him because he's black. Along comes the elderly Bruce Nugent (Robinson) to tell Perry about the days of the Harlem Renaissance in the 1920s, when black, queer artists found a voice for the first time. Nugent flashes back to the days when he collaborated with Langston Hughes (Sunjata), Zora Neale Hurston (Ellis), and others to create the controversial literary magazine *Fire!!* and teaches Perry to find strength in his blackness *and* his gayness, even when those two worlds don't necessarily commingle well.

★ ★

The real Bruce Nugent died in the late '80s, and since Evans's film is set at the beginning of the 21st century, we as an audience have to wrap our brains around the fact that one of the lead characters should, by rights, be in his early hundreds. Even if *Brother to Brother* isn't a perfect film—the reach of this debut feature occasionally exceeds its grasp—it still stands as one of a regrettably few films that attempts to explore the queer black

Duane Boutte (young Bruce Nugent) and Daniel Sunjata (Langston Hughes)

experience. With a few notable exceptions—Jennie Livingston's *Paris Is Burning* (p. 157), Cheryl Dunye's *The Watermelon Woman* (1996), and a handful of titles by Marlon Riggs (including *Tongues Untied*, p. 210), Patrik-Ian Polk, and Isaac Julien—queers of color haven't gotten anything near their due cinematically. But queer festival favorite *Brother to Brother* is by no means a token inclusion in this book—the performances, especially Mackie's and Ellis's, are strong, and the movie importantly touches not only on being a minority within a minority but also on the fact that gays and lesbians need to be cognizant of their history and of the groundbreaking artists and activists of the past who paved the way for where we are today.

CABARET

(1972)

Written by Jay Presson Allen,
based on the musical play by Joe Masteroff,
based on the play *I Am a Camera* by John Van Druten,
based on Christopher Isherwood's *Berlin Stories*.
Directed by Bob Fosse.
Liza Minnelli, Michael York, Joel Grey, Helmut Griem,
Fritz Wepper, Marisa Berenson. (Warner Home Video)

A spiring author Brian Roberts (York) travels to 1930s Berlin to be an English tutor. One of his fellow tenants in his boarding house is American girl Sally Bowles (Minnelli), who sings in a tacky cabaret called the Kit Kat Klub. The two soon begin an affair. Fancying herself a manipulative femme fatale, Sally begins seeing the wealthy aristocrat Maximilian von Heune (Griem). Soon, Brian begins sleeping with Max as well. During their own little personal crises, the Nazi party begins growing more and more powerful, a dominance that is subtly reflected in the onstage goings-on at the Kit Kat.

★ ★

One of the greatest film musicals ever made, Bob Fosse's *Cabaret* brilliantly counterbalances the contextual musical numbers (most of them featuring Joel Grey as the Kit Kat Klub's unforgettably creepy and menacing master of ceremonies) with Germany's slow and inexorable turn towards evil. For an early '70s Hollywood movie, Brian's bisexuality is presented in a very matter-of-fact and inoffensive manner. And then there's Liza—for all the dubious marriages and chemical dependency problems that she's become famous for in recent years, she was still an amazing entertainer. *Cabaret* presents her at her best as an actress *and* as a singer, and even if she never hits those heights again—she came close in Martin Scorsese's *New York, New York* (1977)—she has this movie as an immortal testament to her abilities. We should all have such a snapshot in our wallets.

Quotes to Remember:

> **Sally:** Bri, listen...we're practically living together, so if you only like boys I wouldn't dream of pestering you.
> [*beat*]
> **Sally:** Well, do you sleep with girls or don't you?
> **Brian:** Sally! You don't ask questions like that!
> **Sally:** I do.

> **Sally** [after receiving a cable from her father]: Ten words exactly. After 10 it's extra. You see, Daddy thinks of these things. If I had leprosy, there'd be a cable: "Gee, kid, tough. Sincerely hope nose doesn't fall off. Love."

CAMP

(2003)

Written and directed by Todd Graff.
Daniel 40, Joanna Chilcoat, Robin de Jesus, Alana Allen,
Anna Kendrick, Don Dixon. (MGM Home Entertainment)

A summer camp for high school drama students attracts a motley crew of outsiders, including hetero tease Vlad (Letterle), who longs for attention; nerdy Ellen (Chilcoat), who had to beg her brother to take her to the prom; and queeny, occasionally-cross-dressing Michael (De Jesus), whose parents ignore him. Over the course of the summer, kids will fall in and out of love and friendship, two teen divas (Allen and Kendrick) will battle it out, and a washed-up composer (Dixon) will rediscover his love for music (even if his love for booze remains unabated).

★ ★

Given how clichéd and sappy *Camp* could have been, it turned out wonderfully. Graff's sprightly writing and directing, coupled with an ebulliently talented young cast, magically makes the whole thing work, even the subplot about bitter alcoholic composer Bert Hanley finding redemption at the hand of his young charges. Few films have addressed what it's like to be a gay teenager or a drama club freak, and this movie brilliantly nails the excitement of finding a crew of fellow weirdos who will appreciate and support you. Even after repeated viewings, this movie cracks me up, makes me cry, and gives me the tingles during the incredibly entertaining musical numbers. The big "Turkey-Lurkey Time" sequence (from *Promises! Promises!*) is better than anything in *Chicago* (2002) or almost any other recent screen musical, and it's a real shame that *Camp*'s one original song, the powerful "Here's Where I Stand," didn't get a Best Song Oscar nomination. But even if you're not a theater person, you can't fail to love any film that saves its big movie-star entrance for Stephen Sondheim, who makes a cameo appearance as himself.

Quotes to Remember:

[Here's a joke that separates the theater queens from the civilians]
Jill: Is this your first summer?
Fritzi: No, I was here last year. Remember? We did *'night, Mother* together.
Jill: Oh.

[While the kids on the camp-bound bus are singing Sondheim's "Losing My Mind"]
Bud (introducing himself): Bud Miller, sports counselor.
Patrick: *We* have a *sports counselor*?
Bud: Of course we do. You gonna play some softball this summer?
Patrick: No.

[Fritzi has just poisoned Jill and appears backstage, in costume, ready to go in Jill's place]
Bert: What in the hell are you doing here?
Fritzi: I knew you'd be discussing stopping the show, and I just thought how disappointed all the kids would be.
Bert: You scheming little bitch!
Fritzi: Please! I'm a child.
Bert: If you think for one...

Fritzi: Oh, save the speech, rummy. She's fucked, I'm ready, and the goddamn show must go on. So let's get cracking, shall we?

Bert: Who are you people? What planet did you beam down from? I'm serious. If I can teach you one thing, which is supposed to be my job here, it'd be that you should all go home. Michael Bennett's dead. Bob Fosse is *dead*. Times Square is a theme park now. I hate to be the Grinch, but it's not normal what goes on up here. Somebody has got to warn you. Teenage fag hags become adult fag hags. Straight boys are straight; you can't turn 'em just because you need to be loved. The foundation that's being laid here is not going to help you in the real world. It's going to lead to waitressing jobs and bitterness and the obsessive, pointless collecting of out-of-print original cast albums.

CAN'T STOP THE MUSIC

(1980)

Written by Bronte Woodard and Allan Carr.
Directed by Nancy Walker.
The Village People, Valerie Perrine, Steve Guttenberg,
Bruce Jenner, Marilyn Sokol, June Havoc,
Paul Sand, Barbara Rush, Tammy Grimes.
(Anchor Bay Home Entertainment)

t's the story of the formation of the disco supergroup the
Village People! Only it's not! Retired supermodel Samantha
Simpson (Perrine) helps out her platonic roommate, strug-
gling songwriter Jack Morell (Guttenberg), by putting
together a group of singers to perform his songs. Along the way,
she falls in love with stuffy lawyer Ron (Jenner), who's just
moved from St. Louis to New York City to make his life more
freewheeling. Jack and the band—who, for reasons never really
explained in the movie, dress like different gay fantasy figures—
all get contracts with record mogul Steve Waits (Sand).

★ ★

Oh, you can stop it all right. Where to begin—does one discuss the fact that the disco phenomenon of the late 1970s had gone the way of the dodo by the time this stinker hit theaters? Does one examine the filmmaking style of first- (and last-) time director Nancy "Quicker Picker-Upper" Walker? Perhaps one might parse the horrific performances, the puerile script, or the embarrassing choreography? No, let's jump right to the fact that gay überproducer Allan Carr (*Grease*, 1978) made a movie about a gay disco group that sang songs about gay destinations like San Francisco, Fire Island, the Navy, and the YMCA, yet managed to have that movie be completely free of any actual gay content. (Barring, of course, the Busby-Berkeley-in-Speedos choreography and quick glimpses of cock we get in the film's "YMCA" number. One can only imagine how queer Bruce Vilanch's first draft of the script was.) None of the Village People have love lives, although women are occasionally placed around them in the hopes that we'll think they might be girlfriends. The movie instead centers on the ridiculously contrived romance between polar opposites Samantha and Ron, who have only utter dullness in common. What gayness does sneak into the movie is all via subtext and innuendo. (See Quotes to Remember.) Still, *Can't Stop the Music* is a must-see for its complete insanity, not to mention its inability to predict the effect of AIDS and Ronald Reagan on 1970s gay culture.

Quotes to Remember:

Jack (to Samantha): Anyone who can swallow two Sno Balls and a Ding Dong shouldn't have any trouble with pride!

Jack's mother: It's your music that's bringing all these talented boys together. They ought to get down on their knees...
Jack: Mom!

CARRIE

(1976)

Written by Larry Cohen,
based on the novel by Stephen King.
Directed by Brian De Palma.
Sissy Spacek, Piper Laurie, Nancy Allen, William Katt,
Amy Irving, P.J. Soles, John Travolta, Betty Buckley,
Edie McClurg. (MGM Home Entertainment)

Carrie (Spacek), a shy and quiet girl, is ignored or tormented by her high school classmates. At home, she is persecuted by her fiercely religious mother, Margaret (Laurie), who locks Carrie into a small "prayer closet" as punishment. Around the time Carrie comes to realize that she has telekinetic powers, her classmate Sue (Irving) asks her boyfriend, Tommy (Katt), to take Carrie to the prom as a way of making up for how cruel Sue's friends, particularly Chris (Allen), have been to Carrie. A reluctant Carrie agrees to go, not knowing that Chris has arranged for Carrie to be voted prom queen so that she'll be standing onstage while Chris dumps a bucket of pig's blood on Carrie. But revenge is sweetest when you can fuck people up with your mind.

★ ★

A lot of gay men fiercely identify with this movie, and it's not hard to see why: An ostracized teen with a secret. A batty religious mother who thinks that the child's secret "difference" is a curse from the devil. Obnoxious popular kids who make the heroine's life hell. Ineffectual school officials who are of no help whatsoever. A satisfying bout of revenge in which the misfit gets to destroy the entire high school. (This was back when high school massacres could be presented fictionally without reminding people of reality.) Heck, there's even a scene where Carrie goes to the library to read about her secret strangeness. (Most of us went there to look up *homosexuality* rather than *telekinesis*, but the general feeling is the same.) As far as metaphorical coming-out-of-the-closet movies go, *Carrie* is right up there with *Yentl* (1983), also starring Amy Irving, in which Barbra Streisand (in man drag) has to keep her love for Mandy Patinkin hidden, lest people discover her secret.

Quotes to Remember:

> **Margaret:** Witch! You've got Satan's power!
> **Carrie:** It's nothing to do with Satan, momma. It's me. Me.

CASABLANCA

(1942)

Written by Julius J. Epstein, Philip G. Epstein, and Howard Koch,
based on the play *Everybody Comes to Rick's*
by Murray Burnett and Joan Alison.
Directed by Michael Curtiz.
Humphrey Bogart, Ingrid Bergman, Claude Rains, Paul Henreid, Peter
Lorre, Sydney Greenstreet, Conrad Veidt. (Warner Home Video)

D uring World War II, police captain Louis Renault
(Rains) is madly in love with saloon keeper Rick
Blaine (Bogart); even though the two of them share
trashy dames, Renault's affection for Rick is obvious
from the way he calls him "Ricky" and flits about him, mothlike,
desperate to glean any good gossip about Rick's mysterious past.
One day, Rick's old girlfriend Ilsa (Bergman) shows up in town
with her new man, Victor (Henreid). Can Louis send her packing
so that he can go off into the night with Rick? They'll always
have *Casablanca*.

★ ★

OK, I know, that's not the real plot of this perfect little gem
of the Hollywood studio era. But after repeated viewings, I realized that the real love story going on here is between big, bad,
butch Rick and the obviously-besotted Capt. Renault, who does
everything but giggle and blush when he's in his beloved's presence. And does Rick wind up with the girl at the film's famous
climax? Hell, no. "Louis," Bogart famously drawls. "I think this is
the beginning of a beautiful friendship." Which, for 1942, must

have been code for something else entirely.

Quotes to Remember:

> **Louis,** on Rick:
> (to Rick): You were never interested in *any* woman.

> (to Ilsa, about Rick): He's the kind of man, that, well, if I were a woman, and *I* were not around, I should be in love with Rick.

> (to Rick, about Ilsa): She was asking questions about you earlier, Rick, in a way that made me extremely jealous. [You have to hear Claude Rains's pronunciation of those last two words. Trust me.]

> **Rick** (when asked what kind of man Louis is): Like any other man, only more so.

> **Louis:** Why do you interfere with my little romances?
> **Rick:** Put it down as a gesture to love.

THE CELLULOID CLOSET

(1995)

Written by Rob Epstein, Jeffrey Friedman, and Sharon Wood;
narration written by Armistead Maupin;
based on the book by Vito Russo.
Directed by Rob Epstein and Jeffrey Friedman.
Narrated by Lily Tomlin. (Sony Pictures Home Entertainment)

This fascinating history of gay and lesbian representation in American movies combines clips that span the silent era to the end of the 20th century as well as interviews with such cinema legends as Shirley MacLaine and Tom Hanks and literary lions like Gore Vidal and Susie Bright.

★ ★

A tasty treat for movie lovers, gay or otherwise. By turns hilarious, enraging, enlightening, and encouraging, this look back at queer cinema from Thomas Edison to Gregg Araki and beyond is never less than compelling. Whether it's Susan Sarandon sharing her memories about *The Hunger* (1983) or *Thelma & Louise* (1991) or Gore Vidal revealing how he slipped gay subtext in the Roman epic *Ben-Hur* (1959), *The Celluloid Closet* deftly mixes movie clips—many of them exceedingly obscure but still fascinating—with captivating talking-head interviews. Like the landmark Vito Russo book that inspired it, this film recalls the highs and lows of how queer characters have been presented in (or excluded from) the movies. I'd go so far as to say that if you've never seen *The Celluloid Closet*, you should rent it before watching any of the other movies listed here.

AUTEUR ALERT:

Documentarians Rob Epstein and Jeffrey Friedman have created some of the most compelling nonfiction films about gay life of anyone working today. Other must-sees from this pair include *Paragraph 175* (2000), about gay men who survived the holocaust; *The Times of Harvey Milk* (1984), about the life and death of the influential San Francisco politician; and *Common Threads: Stories From the Quilt* (1989), which examines some of the stories—including Russo's—behind the panels of the NAMES Project AIDS Quilt. (The latter two won Best Documentary Oscars.)

See Also:

Jenni Olson's compilation *Homo Promo* (1993), which captures coming-attractions trailers for queer-themed films of yore. It would appear that the only thing tougher than making movies about gays and lesbians was selling them to the general public, if these bizarre and fascinating ads are to be believed.

CHASING AMY

(1997)

Written and directed by Kevin Smith.
Ben Affleck, Joey Lauren Adams, Jason Lee, Dwight Ewell,
Jason Mewes, Kevin Smith. (Criterion Collection)

Comic book artist Holden McNeil (Affleck) falls for fellow cartoonist Alyssa Jones (Adams) but is dismayed to discover that she's a lesbian. They nonetheless become good friends and start spending time together, much to the consternation of Holden's best friend and comics partner, Banky Edwards (Lee). One night, Holden tells Alyssa that, while he knows they can never be together, he loves her anyway. She yells at him and runs off in the rain but quickly returns and kisses him. Banky foresees disaster for the relationship. Eventually, the two break up not because of Alyssa's orientation but because Holden can't help feeling jealous of her infinitely more experienced sexual past. Holden's friend Silent Bob (Smith) tells him not to be an ass and to appreciate the fact that, even with all her past experience, she has chosen to be with Holden. Holden devises what he thinks will be the solution to his problems with both Alyssa and Banky, but things don't work out as he'd hoped.

★ ★

When I first saw this movie at Sundance in 1997, it totally knocked me out. I'd never seen a movie so smart and so funny about how gay people and straight people relate to each other. Particularly interesting is the character of Hooper X (Ewell), a gay African-American comics creator who has to assume a black militant pose to be taken seriously by his readers. Hooper often winds up being the voice of wisdom in the movie while also rattling off a series of very funny one-liners in an unapologetically queeny way. The fact that a lesbian gets involved with a man in this film ticks off certain quarters of the queer audience to this day, but I think Smith is actually ahead of the game by suggesting that orientation can, in some cases, be fluid and that sometimes people can fall in love with one person in particular even if that person doesn't happen to be of the "right" gender. I, for one, completely buy that Alyssa, while not abandoning her lesbian identity, could fall in love with this specific man. (Much more than I bought it in *Gigli*, where lesbian mobster Jennifer Lopez falls for Affleck. But that's another book.)

Quotes to Remember:

Hooper: Archie was the bitch and Jughead was the butch. That's why he was always going around wearing that crown-looking hat...he was the king of Queen Archie's world.

Banky: What difference does it make if I refer to her as a dyke? Or if I call the Whalers a bunch of faggots in the comfort of my own office, far from the sensitive ears of the rest of the world?

Alyssa: You know, I didn't just heed what I was taught: men and women should be together, it's the natural way, that kind of thing. I'm not with you because of what family, society, life tried to instill in me from day one. The way the world is, how seldom it is that you meet that one person who just gets you—it's so rare. My parents didn't really have it. There were no examples set for me in the world of male-female relationships. And to cut oneself off from finding that person, to immediately halve your options by eliminating the possibility of finding that one person within your own gender, that just seemed stupid to me. So I didn't. But then you came along. You, the one least likely. I mean, you were a *guy*.

Holden: Still am.

AUTEUR ALERT:

While Kevin Smith is straight, he's got a gay brother and an endless fascination and curiosity about sex in general. As a result, all of his films have some kind of queer content, whether it's speculation about the real relationship between his "hetero life-partner" mascots Jay and Silent Bob or blow job jokes that catch you by surprise. (OK, except for *Jersey Girl* (2004), but that film at least features segments from Stephen Sondheim's *Sweeney Todd*.) All of his films are worth checking out, but if you enjoy *Chasing Amy*, make sure to catch *Jay and Silent Bob Strike Back* (2001), which features a clever coda to Banky's homophobia.

CHUCK & BUCK

(2000)

Written by Mike White.
Directed by Miguel Arteta.
Mike White, Chris Weitz, Lupe Ontiveros, Beth Colt,
Paul Weitz. (Artisan Home Entertainment)

Man-child Buck (White) finds himself rocketed into the real world when his invalid mother dies. His boyhood best friend, Chuck (Chris Weitz)—whose juvenile games with Buck initiated both of them into sex—comes to the funeral. Now a music exec who goes by "Charlie," he arrives with his fiancée Carlyn (Colt), and Buck tries to make out with him in the bathroom. A freaked-out Charlie departs, but Buck decides to sell the house and move to Los Angeles, where Charlie and Carlyn live. Charlie realizes that Buck is stalking them, so he insists that Buck stay away. Buck writes a play called *Hank and Frank* and stages it at a children's theater across the street from Charlie's office with the help of seen-it-all stage manager Beverly (Ontiveros), who calls the play a "homoerotic misogynistic love story." Charlie and Carlyn come to see the play, and after some surprising interactions, Buck, Charlie, and Carlyn finally resolve their differences.

★ ★

You've got to admire any movie that gives you a somewhat creepy and developmentally arrested gay stalker—and makes him the *protagonist*. Out writer-star White (best known for his work on cult TV classics like *Freaks and Geeks* and *Pasadena*) makes no effort to put the audience at ease. Buck gets himself into appallingly embarrassing situations—trying to lie his way past a receptionist, showing up unexpectedly outside of restaurants—but the character isn't there for us to mock; we wind up identifying with him just enough to squirm when he says or does the absolute wrong thing. Buck is kind of like the talk-show host–obsessed Rupert Pupkin character in *The King of Comedy* (1983), only it's not fame he's after—he just wants a little TLC from Chuck-Charlie. Chris Weitz goes out on a limb with the character, far enough to freak out audiences who were ready to paint him as just a victim of Buck's obsession. Weitz's real-life brother Paul hilariously plays a terrible actor whom Buck casts in *Hank and Frank* because of his resemblance to Chuck. And while White is riveting throughout, playing one of the cinema's most disturbing and yet sympathetic heroes, Ontiveros steals nearly every scene with her deadpan humor. In a just world, she would play the world-weary sidekick on a hit sitcom who wins Emmys year after year for taking the piss out of the overpaid series star.

Quotes to Remember:

Beverly (to Buck, having just read *Hank and Frank*): I don't think this is a children's play. It's very out there. I think you have something weird about women. I think you have something weird about *men*. How old are you?

Buck (to Charlie): Remember those games we used to play?

Fun Facts:

★ Most of the actors in the film are best known for their work behind the camera: In addition to White's background as a writer for TV and film (*School of Rock*, 2003), Colt is a producer (*Star Maps* (1997), the previous film from Chuck director Arteta), and the Weitz brothers have written, produced and/or directed such hits as *American Pie* (1999), *Antz* (1998), *About a Boy* (2002), and *In Good Company* (2004).

★ Chris and Paul Weitz are third-generation Hollywood—their grandmother is legendary Mexican film star Lupita Tovar, who came to Los Angeles to film the Spanish-language version of the horror classic *Dracula* (1931). At Universal she met and fell in love with studio executive Paul Kohner, who later became agent to such legends as Billy Wilder and Greta Garbo. Paul and Lupita's daughter is Susan Kohner, who starred in *Freud* (1962) opposite Montgomery Clift and in the Douglas Sirk remake of *Imitation of Life* (1959). Chris and Paul are the children of Susan Kohner and fashion designer Jon Weitz.

★ Speaking of previous generations, the openly bisexual Mike White is the son of gay activist Mel White, whose organization Soulforce fights antigay religious oppression.

CRUISING

(1980)

Written by William Friedkin,
based on the novel by Gerald Walker.
Directed by William Friedkin.
Al Pacino, Paul Sorvino, Karen Allen, Richard Cox,
Don Scardino. (VHS only; Warner Home Video)

After a string of unsolved murders in New York's gay leather S/M community, Captain Edelson (Sorvino) sends policeman Steve Burns (Pacino) undercover. Burns gets deeper and deeper into the leather scene, although it causes tensions in his relationship with girlfriend Nancy (Allen). Eventually, he nabs the man responsible for one of the murders, although it's clear that the suspect didn't commit all of them. Steve's gay neighbor is found dead—could the cop have become a killer himself?

★ ★

Probably the most controversial gay film ever made, there's a lot to love and to loathe about *Cruising*. On the plus side, it's a taut, gritty urban thriller that provides an interesting look at the pre-AIDS fetish scene in New York City. At the same time, however, it's often exploitative and vile. (The film's opening title card, which says the film "is not intended as an indictment of the homosexual world," might as well read, "Bring on the freak show!") Friedkin gives us leather drag hookers and a tall black cop who walks into interrogations clad only in a cowboy hat and jock strap, and you begin to wonder on what planet this movie is set. While *Cruising* pays lip service to the fact that the police don't particularly care about the gay murders and want to just nab someone, *anyone*, so that the public will calm down, the film also seems to imply that hanging around these filthy queers is making Pacino's character go gay as well. When we see Allen put on Pacino's leather jacket and motorcycle-cop shades at the end, the implication is that perversion infects everyone it touches. *Cruising* has its queer defenders, and I wind up going back and forth myself over what I think the movie is trying to say and do. But it's provocative enough to merit a look so you can decide for yourself. Whether you find it riveting or abominable, the film won't leave you cold.

Quotes to Remember:

> **Nancy:** Is it me? Are you turned off to me?
> **Steve:** No.
> **Nancy:** Why don't you want me anymore?
> **Steve:** I'm tired, that's all.
> **Nancy:** I'm not an idiot.
> **Steve:** Nance, what I'm doing, it's affecting me.

> **Stuart** (as the two are in the park, undressing):
> How big are you?
> **Steve:** Party size.
> **Stuart:** What are you into?
> **Steve:** I go anywhere.
> **Stuart:** I don't do anything.
> **Steve:** That's cool. Hips or lips?

Fun facts:

> ★ Friedkin edits in subliminal clips of gay anal sex during the first murder scene. He used similar subliminal effects to shock

audiences in *The Exorcist* (1973).

★ Yes, that's young Ed O'Neill (of *Married...With Children* fame) as one of the cops.

★ Al Pacino's spazzy dancing is one of the funniest things you'll ever see.

See Also:

Lesbians also got the chance to be offended in 1980 with the truly tasteless *Windows*, which stars Elizabeth Ashley as a stalker who tries to drive Talia Shire into her arms by hiring a man to brutalize her. Unlike *Cruising*, *Windows* isn't defensible in the slightest. And believe it or not, *Cruising* inspired a "comic" remake, *Partners* (1981). Of the two, *Cruising* is funnier.

THE CRYING GAME

(1992)

Written and directed by Neil Jordan.
Stephen Rea, Jaye Davidson, Miranda Richardson,
Forest Whitaker, Jim Broadbent. (Miramax Home Entertainment)

A squad of Irish Republican Army members kidnap British soldier Jody (Whitaker) in an attempt to force a hostage exchange. During his imprisonment, Jody becomes chummy with Fergus (Rea), one of his captors. Jody tries to escape from Fergus but gets hit by a British army tank moments before squadrons of soldiers shoot up the IRA hideout. Fergus flees to England and, keeping a promise he made, looks up Jody's "special friend" Dil (Davidson), a hairdresser. The two become smitten with each other until Dil reveals, much to Fergus's initial revulsion, that she is transgender. Just as Fergus begins getting his mind around his relationship with Dil, to whom he is still somewhat attracted, some fellow IRA survivors show up to force Fergus to take on one last mission.

★ ★

Before *The Sixth Sense* (1999), *The Crying Game* was a textbook case of how to get people into theaters by generating not only good word-of-mouth but also letting audiences know they needed to go see the movie *immediately* before someone ruined the secret for them. I was lucky enough to see the film in its second day of release in Los Angeles, before anyone was talking about it yet, and I still remember how shocked I was when the camera slowly panned down Dil's body and revealed a penis. But even after you know that Jaye Davidson is a man, *The Crying Game* holds up for repeat viewings, thanks to the quirky script (which combines pyrotechnics with unusual characters and dialogue) and the memorable performances. It's interesting that audiences wound up being receptive to the fact that Rea's character remains taken with Dil even after he discovers what's going on below his lover's waist. Just like Alfred Hitchcock's *Psycho* (1960), *The Crying Game*'s twists can never have the same punch they had during the film's original release, but there's still enough going on here to make the movie a classic that will endure.

Quotes to Remember:

Jody (whose hands are tied, asking Fergus to take his penis out so he can urinate): It's only a piece of meat.

Dil: Funny the way things go—never the way you expect.

Mr. Deveroux (Fergus's obnoxious yuppie boss, who refers to his Irish employee as "Pat," sees Dil approaching): Ah, it's Pat's tart. Does Pat have a tart?
Fergus: She's not a tart.
Mr. Deveroux: Oh, of course not, she's a *lady*.
Fergus: No, she's not that either.

DOG DAY AFTERNOON

(1975)

Written by Frank Pierson,
based on an article by P.F. Kluge and Thomas Moore.
Directed by Sidney Lumet.
Al Pacino, John Cazale, Charles Durning, James Broderick,
Chris Sarandon. (Warner Home Video)

Sonny (Pacino) and Sal (Cazale) try to perpetrate a simple bank robbery in Brooklyn. Everything goes massively wrong: There's hardly any money in the safe, the cops show up, and the TV cameras turn the whole event into a media circus. Things get further complicated when it's discovered that Sonny planned the robbery to pay for a sex-change operation for his "wife" Leon (Sarandon). (Technically, Sonny's a bigamist since he's got a female wife and two kids as well.)

★ ★

The whole "media circus" aspect of *Dog Day Afternoon* hasn't aged well at all—after the O.J. trial, all bets are off as to what constitutes a real-life tragedy that *wouldn't* have TV cameras swarming all around it. But the film still retains a certain power. For one thing, it's young, attractive Pacino at the height of his early powers, unapologetically playing a gay character who professes that he loves Leon "more than any man has ever loved another man." What's also funny—and still true—about the movie's depiction of media coverage is that, once people find out Sonny is gay, the local news stations immediately start covering the event as being "two homosexuals" robbing a bank. The eventual appearance of activists showing up at the crime scene yelling, "Out of the closets and into the streets!" is a nice little snapshot of 1972, when this real-life incident actually happened.

Quotes to Remember:

[After Sonny has been assured he'll be let off lightly if he surrenders]
Sonny: Kiss me.
Detective Moretti: What?
Sonny: When I'm being fucked, I like to get kissed on the mouth.

EDWARD II

(1991)

**Written by Derek Jarman, Ken Butler, Steve Clark-Hall,
Stephen McBride, Antony Root,**
based on the play by Christopher Marlowe.
Directed by Derek Jarman.
Steven Waddington, Andrew Tiernan, Tilda Swinton,
John Lynch, Jerome Flynn. (VHS only; New Line Home Video)

This singularly unorthodox adaptation of the
Christopher Marlowe play tells the story of the British
king Edward II (Waddington) who was destroyed by his
enemies over his relationship with his childhood lover,
Piers Gaveston (Tiernan).

★ ★

Jarman recasts the Marlowe tragedy in contemporary drag,
drawing parallels between Edward's travails and the political
scene of the early 1990s, where queer activists in Britain were
fighting Section 28, a statute barring the "promotion" of homosexuality, which was basically being used to erase anything gay
from the culture. Even though Jarman clearly portrays Edward
as letting his personal life get in the way of being a good king—
and Gaveston as something of a climber—the director makes the
story both sexy and poignant. The always-formidable Tilda
Swinton, swanning about in gorgeous couture, makes Queen
Isabella both victim and monster. Almost no other filmmakers at
the time were making movies so politically ferocious and bla-

tantly sexual—I remember how very exciting this movie was in 1991, and it's lost little of its impact over the years.

Quotes to Remember:

Edward: Ere my sweet Gaveston shall part from me, this isle shall fleet upon the ocean.

Peer of the Realm: Why should you love him who the world hates so?
Edward: Because he loves me more than all the world.

Gaveston: My lord, I hear it whispered everywhere that I am to be banished.
Edward: 'Tis true, sweet Gaveston. Thou must from hence, or I will be deposed. Sweet friend, take it patiently, my love shall never decline.
Gaveston: Is all my hope turned to this hell of grief?
Edward: Rend not my heart with too-piercing words, thou from this land I from myself am banished.
Gaveston: Seeing I must go, do not renew my sorrow.
Edward: Was ever a king so overruled as I? The time is little thou has to stay, and therefore give me leave to look my fill.
Gaveston: 'Tis something to be pitied of a king.

Kent (Edward's brother, to Isabella): Let him without controlment have his will. The mightiest kings have had their minions. Great Alexander loved Hephaestion. The conquering Hercules for Hylas wept, and for Patroclus stern Achilles drooped. And not kings only, but the wisest men—the Roman Tully loved Octavius; grave Socrates, wild Alcibiades. Then let his grace, whose youth is flexible and promiseth as much as we can wish, freely enjoy that vain light-headed Earl, for riper years will wean him from such toys.

Tilda Swinton (Isabella) and John Lynch (Spencer)

Fun facts:

★ The gay activists in the film are actual members of the British group OutRage! Since the organization is a nonviolent one, it was insisted upon that the activists all be defeated by the palace guards.

★ Before singing Cole Porter's "Every Time We Say Goodbye" in *Edward II*, Annie Lennox recorded it for the AIDS fund-raising album *Red Hot and Blue*. The video for the song was directed by Derek Jarman.

★ The poet who reads Dante's *Inferno* to Edward and Gaveston is played by out actor Allan Corduner, who went on to star in such films as Mike Leigh's *Topsy-Turvy* (1999).

AUTEUR ALERT:

While this is probably the most narratively cogent of his films, the often-oblique Derek Jarman is one of the cinema's most important queer directors. This filmmaker-essayist-gardener achieves a kind of poetry through his work, and his creations were always unabashedly gay. *Edward II* sees Jarman raging both against a "heteroppressive" society and against the dying of the light, as he was deep into his struggle against AIDS at this point. (A back-up director had to take over on certain days of the shoot when Jarman was too ill to come to work.) After this film he would make only two more features—the philosophical biography *Wittgenstein* and the all-sounds-no-images *Blue* (both 1993). But all of his films—particularly *Caravaggio* (1986) and *Sebastiane* (1976)—and books are worth a look.

8
WOMEN

(2002)

Written by François Ozon and Marina de Van,
based on the play by Robert Thomas.
Directed by François Ozon.
Catherine Deneuve, Isabelle Huppert, Fanny Ardant,
Emmanuelle Béart, Danielle Darrieux, Firmine Richard,
Ludivine Sagnier, Virginie Ledoyen. (Universal Home Video)

Suzon (Ledoyen) returns home from school at Christmastime only to discover that her dear father has been stabbed. Because of a snowstorm and a cut phone wire, everyone is trapped in the house, which allows younger sister Catherine (Sagnier) to investigate. It appears that everyone in the house had a motive, from the man's cheating wife (Deneuve) to his chambermaid-slash-mistress (Béart) to his insolent sister (Ardant). But not only do all eight women seemingly have both motive and opportunity for murder—they each get a musical number as well.

★ ★

This crazy-quilt combination of *The Women* (see p. 233), *Clue*, and *The Umbrellas of Cherbourg* (1964) was a huge hit in France, thanks to its combination of beloved pop songs and an octet of the nation's favorite actresses from the '50s (Darrieux), '60s (Deneuve), '70s (Huppert), '80s (Ardant, Béart), '90s (Richard, Ledoyen), and the aughts (Sagnier). But even if you don't know the tunes or the ladies, Ozon's clever use of colors and costumes—each woman represents a different flower—and the fun whodunit plot make this an entertaining diversion for gay audiences who aren't afraid of subtitles. While some critics thought the film had a misogynist streak, I feel that Ozon is portraying women who are all stuck in unpleasant situations because of the 1950s setting. The story makes salient points about classism (the maids versus the bosses), homophobia (there is much hypocritical gnashing of teeth when one of the women is revealed to be a lesbian), and the trap of having marriage be a woman's only option in life.

AUTEUR ALERT:

> With just a handful of films under his belt, François Ozon is already proving to be one of international cinema's most exciting young queer directors. If you like *8 Women*, give a look to *Swimming Pool* (2003) and *Water Drops on Burning Rocks* (2000)—both also featuring Sagnier—as well as *Criminal Lovers* (1999), *Sitcom* (1998), and his interesting short films, many of which are available on DVD.

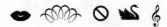

FAR FROM HEAVEN

(2002)

Written and directed by Todd Haynes.
Julianne Moore, Dennis Quaid, Dennis Haysbert,
Patricia Clarkson, Viola Davis, Celia Weston.
(Universal Home Video)

Cathy Whitaker (Moore), a housewife and mother in 1957 Connecticut, seems to have the perfect life—beautiful home, two darling children, and a devoted husband, Frank (Quaid). But, as is so often the case, all is not well beneath the surface: One night when Frank is "working late," Cathy brings his dinner to the office only to find him in the arms of another man. He seeks psychological counseling to "cure" his tendencies but grows further and further distant from Cathy. She finds herself becoming closer to Raymond Deagan (Haysbert), her cultured, gentle gardener. But Cathy's friends and neighbors are scandalized by her close friendship with a black man. Can these three find happiness?

★ ★

On one level, *Far From Heaven* is a rethinking of Douglas Sirk's *All That Heaven Allows* (1955), which stars Jane Wyman as a widow who shocks her spoiled children and gossipy neighbors by entering into a relationship with bohemian landscaper

71

Rock Hudson. But it's not just the consideration of racial and sexual themes that keeps *Far From Heaven* from being merely a remake (or, as some foolishly consider it, a parody) of Sirk. Haynes celebrates not only an essential filmmaker who came before him (Sirk was also a great influence on Rainer Werner Fassbinder—see p. 71), but also the power of melodrama in general. It's easy to sneer at old "women's pictures" for their excesses, but they were rare instances where the stories and problems that women faced in their own lives were explored in the popular culture. Like Haynes's earlier *Safe* (1995), also starring Moore, *Far From Heaven* understands what makes women in certain situations tick, and he confronts the forces that conspire to box them into their roles in life.

AUTEUR ALERT:

> Todd Haynes is one of the most important—and fascinating, and entertaining—filmmakers working today, gay or otherwise. His films often bear the influence of earlier periods and styles, but he is firmly original in his narrative style and visual sensibility. From his outstanding student thesis film, *Superstar: The Karen Carpenter Story* (1987) (which is hard to track down because of copyright issues), to his short film *Dottie Gets Spanked* (1993) to his handful of features, all of Haynes's work is provocative and a must-see. And while you're at it, check out Sirk's great sudsy quartet of *All That Heaven Allows, Imitation of Life* (1959), *Magnificent Obsession* (1954), and *Written on the Wind* (see p. 238).

FEMALE TROUBLE

(1974)

Written and directed by John Waters.
Divine, Mink Stole, David Lochary, Mary Vivian Pearce, Edith Massey,
Cookie Mueller, Susan Walsh. (New Line Home Video)

High school dropout Dawn Davenport (Divine) runs away from home on Christmas Day after she dumps the tree on her parents in retaliation for them not buying her the cha-cha heels she had demanded. Impregnated by the drunk driver (also Divine) who picked her up hitchhiking, Dawn gives birth to her daughter, Taffy, in a squalid hotel. Years later, Dawn and her old school pals Chicklette (Walsh) and Concetta (Mueller) become whores and thieves. Dawn is "discovered" by beauticians Donald (Lochary) and Donna Dasher (Pearce), who believe that "crime makes you more beautiful" and want to photograph Dawn perpetrating various offenses. Ida (Massey), furious at Dawn for marrying and then driving away Ida's nephew Gator, throws acid on her face, but the Dashers tell Dawn that the facial scars make her even more beautiful. Before her big nightclub show, Dawn strangles Taffy (Stole), who has become a Hare Krishna; the climax of the show features Dawn firing a gun into the audience. Betrayed at her murder trial by the Dashers, Dawn goes to the electric chair, but she's thrilled about all the publicity she'll get.

★ ★

Susan Walsh (Chicklette), Divine (Dawn Davenport), Cookie Mueller (Concetta)

Three cheers for John Waters, the crackpot auteur whose outrageous comedies get to the heart of the American experience. While *Female Trouble* retains its ability to shock—when Taffy is born, Dawn chews through her own umbilical cord—the movie's notion of crime-as-publicity-opportunity has become ever more resonant over the years. *Female Trouble* represents the apex of Waters's early career with his Baltimore-based "Dreamland" players, all of whom shine in very bizarre roles. The colossal, outrageous drag performer Divine, of course, is the actor most associated with Waters's early work, and his Dawn Davenport is despicable and riveting at the same time. But even though Waters's later budgets would get bigger, and major stars like Kathleen Turner and Tracey Ullmann would join his casts, his movies continue to be uniquely insane and brilliant.

Quotes to Remember:

Dawn (to young Taffy, who wants to go to school): There is no need to know about the presidents, wars, numbers, or science. Just listen to me, and you'll learn.

Ida: All those beauticians and you don't have any boy dates?
Gator: I don't want any boy dates.
Ida: Oh, honey, I'd be so happy if you'd turn nellie.
Gator: There ain't no way. I'm straight. I mean, I like a lot of queers, but I don't dig their equipment, you know? I like women.
Ida: But you could change. Queers are just better. I'd be so proud if you was a fag and had a nice beautician boyfriend. I'd never have to worry...The world of heterosexuals is a sick and disgusting life!

Donna (to Dawn, commanding): Model! Model!

Dawn (to a fellow death-row inmate): Tell everyone they have my permission to sell their memories of me to the media.

AUTEUR ALERT:

John Waters is an essential filmmaker whose queer sensibilities have molded at least one generation of nonconformists and what *Female Trouble* would call "backsassers" and "shit-starters." Start with *Female Trouble, Hairspray* (1988), *Pink Flamingos* (1972), *A Dirty Shame* (2004), and the underrated *Pecker* (1998), but see everything he's ever done.

FIGHT CLUB

(1999)

Written by Jim Uhls,
based on the novel by Chuck Palahniuk.
Directed by David Fincher.
Edward Norton, Brad Pitt, Helena Bonham-Carter, Meat Loaf,
Jared Leto. (Twentieth Century Fox Home Entertainment)

A harried, insomniac white-collar drone (Norton) crosses paths with devil-may-care soap salesman Tyler
Durden (Pitt), and the two of them discover the joy of
beating each other up. Soon, they have started Fight
Club, an underground organization of men dedicated to reclaim-
ing their masculinity in a world of marketing and Ikea furniture
by gathering in basements to wallop the crap out of each other.
What begins as a purely pugilist exercise works its way up to
creative vandalism and then, ultimately, terrorism. And when
"Jack" (Norton's character is technically nameless, but a running
gag in the film makes "Jack" as good a name for him as any)
finally has to face off with Tyler, he's forced to confront some
uncomfortable truths about himself.

★ ★

Sometimes you have to look at a movie and ask yourself: *Do
the filmmakers have any idea how fucking gay this is?* All the
shirtless bonding and glamorously choreographed scrapping, all
this reclamation of manhood in a world virtually without

women—you expect a Falcon video to break out of this movie at any moment. (If the film's fashion-spread violence isn't gay enough for you, there's also the sight of Helena Bonham-Carter singing the theme from *Valley of the Dolls*. [see p. 216]) But *Fight Club*—based on the novel by gay author Chuck Palahniuk—is exhilaratingly entertaining, smartly art-directed, and superbly acted. It's also a crock of shit. Like an Ayn Rand novel, it raises lots of Big Ideas, only to attempt to resolve them in the most ham-fisted way possible. It's the sort of philosophizing that generates enthusiasm among undergraduates, but the film's destroy-your-credit-cards dogma doesn't hold up to more than five minutes or so of scrutiny. It's hard to decide what's more fatuous—the film's anticelebrity and antivanity message being delivered by the well-paid and aesthetically-endowed Pitt and Norton, or the notion of substance over style being championed in a movie by the visually extravagant David Fincher. Still, given the fear that most studio films have about containing any ideas whatsoever, you have to give *Fight Club* points for trying. And you'll have a great time watching it; just don't adopt it as a manifesto.

Quotes to Remember:

Chuck Palahniuk (on the DVD commentary track, over the scene where Pitt and Norton share a beer after their first fight): Now this is so weird. Drinking out of the same, uh, thing is sort of like a shorthand for a love relationship in so many movies that I couldn't believe they were sharing a beer. It just seemed such a powerful metaphor.

"Jack": Tyler dumped me. I am Jack's broken heart.

FOX AND HIS FRIENDS

(1975)

Written by Rainer Werner Fassbinder and Christian Hohoff.
Directed by Rainer Werner Fassbinder.
Peter Chatel, Rainer Werner Fassbinder, Karlheinz Böhm,
Adrian Hoven. (Wellspring Video)

Carnival worker Franz "Fox" Biberkopf (Fassbinder) loses his gig when his lover (and barker) gets arrested. Fox's luck seems to turn around when he wins the lottery, but unfortunately for him, he falls in with a group of snotty bourgeois faggots. Eugen (Chatel), the son of an industrialist on the verge of bankruptcy, takes Fox as a boyfriend, but it's clear that Eugen, with the help of his obnoxious, class-conscious pals, is out to soak Fox for his money. Fox begins to realize what's going on but makes little effort to save himself, and at the end of the film he's lying dead on a subway station floor, as children pick his pockets and his former friends step over him.

★ ★

OK, when groups like the Gay and Lesbian Alliance Against Defamation (GLAAD) say they want to see "positive" images of homos in movies, I have to wonder what they would make of a film like *Fox and His Friends*, made by a queer auteur, which features a host of thoroughly despicable gay characters. Of course, Fassbinder isn't out to paint all gay people with the same brush, but he's certainly making points about class conflicts. For all the talk of a gay "community," gay men and lesbians are united almost solely by their sexual orientation; as such, the umbrella of queerness covers all races, genders, religions, and classes, which guarantees that things are going to get messy. Privileged white male gays aren't necessarily going to empathize with the struggles of queer African-Americans, women, the poor, or anyone else. And by not trying to sugarcoat that fact, Fassbinder created a devastatingly powerful—and, at times, even painful to watch—drama.

AUTEUR ALERT:

Back in the '70s, when Hollywood was terrified to deal with gay subject matter, Rainer Werner Fassbinder was ragingly out of the closet and utterly unafraid to tell queer stories. He lived a messy life, but managed to crank out some 36 features before his death at 33 of a drug-related suicide. Inspired by the melodramas of Douglas Sirk, Fassbinder told sad, stripped-down stories of all kinds of miserable people. But even if his movies are often a bummer, they're rarely dull and frequently provocative. Start with *Fox, The Marriage of Maria Braun* (1979), and *Ali: Fear Eats the Soul* (1974), his spin on Sirk's All That Heaven Allows.

Aa +/-

FUNNY GIRL

(1968)

Written by Isobel Lennart,
based on her musical play.
Directed by William Wyler.
Barbra Streisand, Omar Sharif, Kay Medford, Anne Francis,
Walter Pidgeon, Mae Questel.
(Sony Pictures Home Entertainment)

Fanny Brice (Streisand) rises up from vaudeville to the prestigious Ziegfeld Follies with her unconventional sense of humor and beautiful singing voice. She loves gambler Nicky Arnstein (Sharif), but her continued success in the face of his mounting financial losses puts a strain on the relationship.

★ ★

What's more tiresome than queens who worship everything Barbra Streisand does? Bitter fags who despise Streisand simply by virtue of the fact that she's a favorite among gay men of a certain age. While she's certainly made her share of dubious artistic choices over the years, Streisand at her best is a force to be reckoned with. It's become fashionable to slag her middlebrow sensibilities, her perceived monstrous ego, and her outspoken politics, but I can't help feeling that she would be forgiven for all three if she were a man. In any event, she rocks the fucking house in *Funny Girl*, her feature film debut that would garner her a Best Actress Oscar. She convincingly plays Brice as both gawky youngster and seasoned sophisticate, naive and jaded, entranced by love and hurt by it. And while she might have butted heads with legendary director William Wyler, the result is a handful of great movie musical numbers, particularly "Don't Rain on My Parade." The film itself isn't always worthy of its star; the subpar *Star Is Born* stuff in the second half is so melodramatic and uninteresting that on repeat viewings, I tend to cut right from the intermission to Streisand's showstopping rendition of "My Man" at the film's climax. If anyone tells me he hates Barbra Streisand, I always ask him if he's seen *Funny Girl* and *What's Up, Doc?* (1972) (her funniest film appearance, and one she barely sings in). If he hasn't, then I don't give him the right to harsh on Babs.

THE GANG'S ALL HERE

(1943)

Written by Walter Bullock,
from a story by Nancy Winter & George Root Jr. and Tom Bridges.
Directed by Busby Berkeley.
Alice Faye, Carmen Miranda, Phil Baker, Benny Goodman, Eugene
Pallette, Edward Everett Horton, James Ellison. (As of this printing,
not yet available from Twentieth Century Fox Home Entertainment)

Chorus girl Edie (Faye) falls in love with Andy (Ellison) just before he ships out to World War II. After he wins a medal for fighting in the South Pacific, his father (Pallette) arranges a party featuring all the talent at Edie's nightclub at the estate of his Westchester, N.Y., neighbor, the uptight Mr. Potter (Horton). Edie is hurt to discover that Andy is supposed to marry the Potters' daughter, but she finds out that the two childhood friends have no real intention to wed.

★ ★

It took *four* writers to come up with this script? Never mind the drearily wholesome Alice Faye romance at the center of this insane Busby Berkeley musical. Berkeley was famous for crafting films that involved hundreds of chorus girls making kaleidoscope shapes or playing neon violins; feast your eyes on the rows of lovelies holding up giant bananas while Carmen Miranda sings "The Lady in the Tutti Frutti Hat." Enjoy Charlotte Greenwood's long legs and wry sense of humor. Gape in disbelief at the crazy elaborateness of the "Polka Dot Polka" number. And then, of course, there's the always-entertaining Horton, one of Hollywood's great sissies. This monument to excess is one-of-a-kind, even among other musicals (or, for that matter, among *Busby Berkeley* musicals). *The Gang's All Here* is the kind of camp hoot enjoyed by our gay ancestors, but certain types of nuttiness never go out of style; see for yourself why one critic hails this classic as "some sort of apotheosis in vulgarity."

THE GAY DECEIVERS

(1969)

Written by Jerome Wish,
from a story by Gil Lasky and Abe Polsky.
Directed by Bruce Kessler.
Kevin Coughlin, Lawrence P. Casey, Michael Greer.
(Image Entertainment)

Law student Danny (Coughlin) and ladies' man Elliot (Casey) pretend to be gay to avoid getting drafted and sent to Vietnam. But the local draft board is keeping an eye on them, so they maintain the ruse by moving into a cottage decorated and maintained by poofylicious landlord Malcolm DeJohn (Greer). Danny's family and girlfriend mistakenly think the two are gay. Not much hilarity ensues.

★ ★

This feeble farce belongs in a time capsule alongside *Bugs Bunny Nips the Nips* and old episodes of *Amos 'n' Andy*. The whole notion of gayness is handled with tongs by the filmmakers who try to caricature all the gay characters while still expressing regret that being gay can get you fired from your job...when it happens to hetero Elliot, anyway. What makes the movie worth seeing is Michael Greer, who single-handedly elevates the film by refusing to be the butt of any straight guy's joke. His

Malcolm is flamboyant and over-the-top, but he owns it, Mary. (So much so that he reportedly rewrote all his own dialogue.) This performance alone ranks Greer as an unsung hero of the Stonewall generation.

Quotes to Remember:

> **Elliot** (realizing the cottage has only one bedroom): It's bad enough I gotta live here in Fairyland, now you want me to share the same bed?
> **Danny**: You're forgetting something—see, we're supposed to live like, uh...lovers.
> **Elliot:** Swell. And what'll we do for a nursery when the little ones come along? [Pretends to pick up the room's foofy French phone and hands it to nude statue] "It's for you, thweetie."

> **Leslie:** That whole scene he's moved into—it's *unhealthy*.

See Also:

Fortune and Men's Eyes (1971), another wretched and exploitive movie about gay themes saved only by the presence of the incomparable Michael Greer.

 **+/-**

THE GAY DIVORCEE

(1934)

**Written by George Marion Jr.,
Dorothy Yost, and Edward Kaufman,**
based on the musical play *The Gay Divorcee*
by Dwight Taylor, Kenneth S. Webb, and Samuel Hoffenstein.
Directed by Mark Sandrich.
Fred Astaire, Ginger Rogers, Alice Brady, Edward Everett Horton,
Erik Rhodes, Eric Blore. (VHS only; Turner Home Video)

Dancer Guy Holden (Astaire) travels to London with his lawyer friend Egbert (Horton). At customs, Guy falls in love with Mimi (Rogers) after he accidentally tears her skirt. Egbert's onetime fiancée Hortense (Brady) brings her niece Mimi to his office so that Egbert can arrange Mimi's divorce. Egbert hires gigolo Tonetti (Rhodes) to be Mimi's fake "correspondent" in the divorce, but Mimi thinks that Guy is the gigolo. Complications ensue.

★ ★

OK, let's just forget the plot. Fred Astaire and Ginger Rogers movies are all about watching the two of them do some of the most breathtaking dancing ever captured on film. For gay audiences, there's the added benefit of a supporting cast full of poofs. What Tony Randall was to Doris and Rock, Edward Everett Horton was to Fred and Ginger. Also along for the ride this time, we have fey butler Eric Blore and prissy gigolo Erik

Rhodes, who tends to favor moustache wax and his concertina over the ladies. Gay humor is an ever-evolving thing, but I always love the antics of these foppish 1930s eunuchs. See for yourself if you don't agree.

Quotes to Remember:

Hortense (about Egbert): He was nearly my third husband. He would have been too, but he suddenly left for India on an elephant hunt. I wonder why he'd prefer to hunt elephants when he could have married me?

Egbert: You're absolutely sure, Mr. Tonetti, that my client will be safe?
Tonetti: Oh, signore, with me, strictly business. My slogan—"Your wife is safe with Tonetti. He prefers spaghetti."

Mimi's husband (not believing she's cheated on him with Tonetti): I'd never believe it was him—this *hairdresser*!

GIANT

(1956)

Written by Fred Guiol and Ivan Moffat,
based on the novel by Edna Ferber.
Directed by George Stevens.
Elizabeth Taylor, Rock Hudson, James Dean, Mercedes McCambridge,
Carroll Baker, Jane Withers, Dennis Hopper. (Warner Home Video)

When Texas cattle rancher Jordan Benedict (Hudson) travels east to Maryland to buy a prize horse, he winds up picking up a bride as well—beautiful, independent, headstrong Leslie (Taylor). While the arid, expansive landscape of Texas is as alien to her as her husband's racism and sexism is appalling, Leslie sets about becoming the lady of the house and mother to their children. Feeling pushed aside, Jordan's sister Luz (McCambridge) gets thrown from a horse and leaves a chunk of the family land to ne'er-do-well Jett Rink (Dean). The land winds up having lots and lots of oil under it, making Jordan's longtime nemesis one of the richest men in the world. As the new generation of Benedicts grows up over the next quarter of a century, they will all see their worlds change and intersect in unexpected ways.

★ ★

This expansive family saga, stretching 25 years from the Depression to the post-World War II era, is the kind of big-budget sudser that the movies have long since left to the TV miniseries and primetime soaps. But no *Thorn Birds or Dynasty* has ever lived up to the blueprints left by this George Stevens

smash. There's not anything explicitly gay going on here, except
for the dykiness that McCambridge brings to almost every role—
her work here barely has a patch on her full-out *Johnny Guitar*
(1954) butchness, though. Nonetheless, it's kind of a thrill to
watch Elizabeth Taylor share the screen with queer film legends
Rock Hudson and James Dean. (Speaking of Taylor, I think
"fairy princess" has a much nicer ring to it than "fag hag.") You
look at the close-ups of the three stars of this film, and you're
reminded of Norma Desmond's line in *Sunset Blvd.* (see p.
202)—"They had *faces* then." An extended shot of Dean from
behind at the beginning of the film reminds us they had *asses*
then too.

GIRLS WILL BE GIRLS

(2003)

Written and directed by Richard Day.
Jack Plotnick, Clinton Leupp, Jeffery Roberson, Ron Mathews,
Dana Gould, Dennis Hensley. (MGM Home Entertainment)

Boozy, washed-up starlet Evie Harris (Plotnick) rattles around her Hollywood mansion with her friend and servant Coco (Leupp), who pines for her one true love—the doctor who performed her abortions several years earlier. The two take in a tenant—Varla (Roberson), an aspiring actress whose mother Marla's star-making role was stolen away from her by Evie. Will Varla find fame and revenge? Will Coco find "Dr. Perfect"? Will Evie remain conscious long enough to relaunch her career with a "specia-mercial"?

★ ★

Both outrageous and restrained, *Girls Will Be Girls* borrows from the classic showbiz melodramas—*All About Eve* (see p. 1), *Valley of the Dolls* (see p. 216), *What Ever Happened to Baby Jane?* (see p. 226)—but still feels fresh and inspired. *Girls Will Be Girls* juggles its characters and plotlines well, giving these talented performers more than just one joke to play over and

Jack Plotnick (background, as Evie) and Clinton Leupp (Coco)

over. The characters actually grow and evolve as human beings while still remaining bizarre and uproarious. Judging from writer-director Day's follow-up effort *Straight-Jacket* (2004), it seems a good bet that the screenplay was very much a collaboration with his leading "ladies." Some of Evie's one-liners will definitely sound familiar to fans of Plotnick and Dennis Hensley's acclaimed Internet short *Evie Harris: Shining Star*. But what makes *Girls* particularly memorable is the fact that all three leads are shrewd enough to deliver the bawdiest of dialogue in the most deadpan style possible.

Quotes to Remember:

> **Evie:** I met Fred MacMurray at the Brown Derby when they were casting *Flubber*, and he threw me a juicy part.
> **Coco:** And then he put you in the picture.

Varla: My mother always said, "Feelings are like treasures. So bury them."

Coco: Have you ever had an abortion, Evie?
Evie: Please. I've had more babies pulled out of me than a burning orphanage.

🦢 🚻 "

GLITTER

(2001)

Written by Kate Lanier,
from a story by Cheryl L. West.
Directed by Vondie Curtis-Hall.
Mariah Carey, Max Beesley, Da Brat,
Tia Texada, Ann Magnuson, Terence Howard.
(Twentieth Century Fox Home Entertainment)

Young Billie Frank is packed off to an orphanage after her alcoholic singer mother burns the house down. All grown up, Billie (Carey) and her friends Roxanne (Texada) and Louise (Da Brat) start dancing in New York City nightclubs in 1983. A shady producer (Howard) hires the trio and uses Billie's vocals to cover up the squawks of his gorgeous but untalented girlfriend. DJ Dice (Beesley) sees Billie's talent and buys her contract. Under Dice's tutelage, Billie becomes a famous singer, but her fame strains their romantic relationship. On the night of her sold-out Madison Square Garden concert, the producer shoots Dice in the street over a business dispute. After the show, she reads a note from Dice telling Billie that her mother has been located, so Billie takes a limo to rural Maryland for a reunion.

★ ★

Words cannot describe how ridiculous this *Star Is Born* rip off is, but I'll give it my best shot: Regrettable. Hacky. Embarrassing. Anyway, let's start with Mariah Carey—even if you're a fan of her vocalizing, there's no denying that the lady can't act. (Based on this movie, anyway: Carey is surprisingly spunky and watchable in *Wisegirls* (2002), so maybe she just needs an acting class or eight to get her up to snuff.) The filmmakers must have realized this early on, because you've never seen someone so inert at the center of a movie. (Watch the big scene where she and Dice go to the record label and find out that they want to sign a contract with Billie. She utters all of one word while everyone around her makes the biggest decision of her life.) There's also the fact that Carey's larger-than-usual eyelids often make her photograph like a Muppet, but that's neither here nor there. Then there's *Glitter*'s version of 1983 club life, which magically lacks any drugs or gay people (except for one drag queen in the background in a single scene). Only the great Ann Magnuson seems to be trying to look or act like this is supposed to be set in the Reagan era. And don't get me started about young Billie's cat, which goes with her to the orphanage and then is magically still alive more than a decade later when she's moving out of Dice's place. Or the scene where Billie's head appears to explode in a shower of happy fireworks. Gay men love their divas, but we also love watching them belly flop, and that's why *Glitter* makes perfect viewing for schadenfreude-minded fags.

GO FISH

(1994)

Written by Guinevere Turner and Rose Troche.
Directed by Rose Troche.
Guinevere Turner, V.S. Brodie, T. Wendy McMillan,
Migdalia Melendez, Anastasia Sharp. (MGM Home Entertainment)

Cute young dyke Max (Turner) is looking for love. Her roomie and onetime college professor, Kia (McMillan), tries to set up Max with Ely (Brodie), a somewhat older and introverted woman who's not traditionally pretty. Max balks at first, but as she and Ely get to know each other, they gradually grow closer. Meanwhile Kia's girlfriend, Evy (Melendez), gets kicked out of her mother's house after her male ex outs her, and the gals' sex-positive pal Daria (Sharp) imagines facing a tribunal of angry lesbians after having sex with a man.

★ ★

This cornerstone of the New Queer Cinema remains fresh and funny and sexy more than a decade after it blew away Sundance audiences who had never seen a lesbian movie quite like this one. Director Rose Troche adds visual flourishes (in her black-and-white film) to the smart, sharp dialogue she wrote with then-girlfriend Turner. The movie's observations about falling in love are universal ones, and the characters are all people you wind up wanting to spend lots more time with. While the film's production woes are now the stuff of legend—Troche and

Turner ran out of money and were only able to finish the film with the help of producer Tom Kalin (*Swoon,* p. 204)—the movie wears its low budget well and holds up as an example of how talent and creativity can trump a shortage of funds. The wave that *Go Fish* began can now be seen every week on Showtime's *The L Word*—a show for which, appropriately enough, Troche and Turner were key architects in its first seasons.

Quotes to Remember:

Kia: Miss Camille West, a.k.a. Max, has this ideal girlfriend in her head. I think it's like Hip-Hop Barbie or something.

Max (writing advice about love in her diary): Don't fear too many things; it's dangerous. Don't say so much; you'll ruin everything. Don't worry yourself into a corner, and just don't think about it so much. The girl you're gonna meet doesn't look like anyone you know, and when you meet her, your toes might tingle or you might suppress a yawn. It's hard to say. Don't box yourself in. Don't leave yourself wide open. Don't think about it every second, but just don't let yourself forget—the girl is out there.

GODS AND MONSTERS

(1998)

Written by Bill Condon,
based on the novel *Father of Frankenstein* by Christopher Bram.
Directed by Bill Condon.
Ian McKellen, Brendan Fraser, Lynn Redgrave,
Lolita Davidovich, Jack Plotnick. (Lions Gate Home Video)

L egendary gay Hollywood filmmaker James Whale (McKellen) is recovering from a stroke and finds that his mind is going in "a hundred directions at once," leading to a constant series of flashbacks: growing up poor in northern England, fighting in the trenches during World War I, directing *The Bride of Frankenstein* (1935) for Universal. Whale becomes smitten with his new gardener, Clay Boone (Fraser), and after some initial awkwardness, the two become friends. But as Whale's mental condition deteriorates, he reveals one final hidden agenda in his friendship with the strapping young man.

★ ★

For his extraordinary performance as an aging artist facing his final destiny, gay actor Ian McKellen did not win the Academy Award, but he managed the next-best thing: losing an Academy Award to Roberto Benigni. I mean, really. In any event, out writer-director Bill Condon's loving biography of James Whale—who made films as varied as *Waterloo Bridge* (1931) and the original *Show Boat* (1936), but who is best remembered for the witty horror classics *Frankenstein* (1931) and its first sequel, *The Old Dark House* (1932), and *The Invisible Man* (1933)—is a truly remarkable film in a number of ways. It's a tart portrait of Hollywood and how the movie machine deals with its discards. It's an understated coming-of-age story (for Clay) played against the portrait of a man who can bear the loss of his physicality but not of his faculties. ("When you die," Whale tells Clay, "make sure that your brain is the last organ to fizzle.")

Quotes to Remember:

Clay: You ever been married, Mr. Whale?

James: No. Well, not in the legal sense.

Clay: What other sense is there?

James: Well, one can live as husband and wife without getting the law involved.

Clay: So then you did have a wife.

James: Or a husband, depending on which of us you asked. My friend David lived here for many years.

Clay: Oh.

James: Does that surprise you?

Clay: No, um...you're a homosexual.

James (flinching): If one must use the clinical name.

Clay: I'm not, you know.

James: I never thought you were.

Clay: You don't think of me that way, do you?

James: And what way would that be?

Clay: Well, the way that I look at women.

James: Oh, don't be ridiculous. I know a real man like you would break my neck if I so much as laid a finger on you. [Puffs on cigar] Besides, you're not my type. [Both laugh]

GREY GARDENS

(1975)

**Directed by David Maysles, Albert Maysles,
Muffie Meyer, Ellen Hovde.**
(Criterion Collection)

This legendary documentary follows the home life of
Edith Bouvier Beale, a relative of Jacqueline Bouvier
Kennedy Onassis, who lives with her 50-ish daughter
"Little Edie"—not to mention countless cats and rac-
coons—in a crumbling estate in the Hamptons.

★ ★

It's hard to sum up the odd humor and rampant bizarreness
of *Grey Gardens* to folks who haven't seen it. Suffice it to say
that it's a very intimate glimpse into the lives of two batty, bick-
ering women who are strangely dependent on each other. At the
same time, however, one gets the impression that the arguments
they're having on camera about past regrets are the same fights
they've had (and will go on having) for years. Of particular interest is Little Edie, who is given to very unique outfits, all of
which feature some sort of head wrap pinned with a jeweled
brooch—the wrap itself can be anything from a silk scarf to
twisted-up cardigan to a beach towel, but she makes the look
her own. No wonder gay fashionistas like Todd Oldham and
John Bartlett turn up on the DVD to pay homage to her incredibly strange stylishness.

Quote to Remember:

Little Edie: But, you see, in dealing with me, the relations didn't know that they were dealing with a *staunch* character. And I tell you, if there's anything worse than a staunch woman—S-T-A-U-N-C-H. There's nothing worse, I'm telling you. They don't weaken, no matter what.

GRIEF

(1993)

Written and directed by Richard Glatzer.
Craig Chester, Illeana Douglas, Alexis Arquette, Kent Fuher
(a.k.a. "Jackie Beat"), Carlton Wilborn, Lucy Gutteridge,
Mickey Cottrell, Katherine Connella, Jeffrey Hilbert. (TLA Home Video)

The real drama on the "grade-Z" TV show *The Love Judge* is going on behind the scenes: Mark (Chester) is dealing with the anniversary of his lover's death and trying to decipher the flirty signals from straight-boy Bill (Arquette), who's having a clandestine affair with Jeremy (Wilborn) on the office couch owned by Jo (Fuher), the executive producer who's about to quit and go to Prague and will hand the reins over to either Mark or Paula (Gutteridge). Meanwhile, Jo's goofy assistant Leslie (Douglas) is trying to get on both the writing staff *and* the cute copier repairman.

★ ★

Gay people in the movies have lovers, families, and crises, but they rarely ever seem to have jobs. And if they do, their 9-to-5 hours barely register in the plot. But *Grief* is more than just a great workplace comedy—it's a celebration of friendship and camaraderie, and of how we sometimes need the people around us to get us through another day and keep us from jumping off a roof. If I ran Hollywood, this movie would be the pilot to a great long-running sitcom about the oddball staff of a terrible daytime TV show. As it is, it's a showcase for terrific performances, particularly from Kent Fuher-Jackie Beat, who is both sardonically deadpan and surprisingly touching. (He gets an amazing speech about how when Jo walks into a room, "fat" is all anyone sees.) His character Jo, incidentally, is a woman and not a drag queen, which puts Fuher's perfectly understated performance right up there with Linda Hunt's Oscar-winning cross-dressing in *The Year of Living Dangerously* (1982) as far as I'm concerned.

Quotes to Remember:

Jo (in a staff meeting): Can we have a little less magazine reading and a little more me?

Leslie: Hey, I have an idea. Why don't you and I get married? Come on, I'm proposing to you. The hell with everyone, we can have a great apartment and we'll throw fabulous Christmas parties every year. We can be like one of those phony couples you always see in *House and Garden* magazine. You know, showing off their Stickley furniture and then they always talk about how they collect vintage pocketbooks from flea markets and stuff.
Mark: Right, and I can write children's books.
Leslie: Yeah, you write children's books, and I'll be press secretary for Tipper Gore.

Mark: I was going to resign today.
Jo: Great.
Mark: I was thinking...and I don't think I want to work for those scumbags anymore.
Jo: Excuse me, are there any other scumbags offering you a paycheck?
Mark: No.
Jo: Yeah. Then I guess they win, huh?

Craig Chester, Illeana Douglas, Carlton Wilborn

See Also:

Late Bloomers (1996), another great workplace comedy, about a female coach and a teacher's wife whose clandestine lesbian affair rocks their small Texas high school.

HAPPY TOGETHER

(1997)

Written and directed by Wong Kar-Wai.
Leslie Cheung, Tony Leung, Chang Chen. (Kino Home Video)

Traveling Hong Kong natives Fai (Leung) and Po (Cheung) are stuck in Argentina, and their on-again-off-again relationship is off. Fai gets a job as a greeter at a tango bar while Po shows up with a series of shady boyfriends. After Po is severely beaten (for stealing a watch from a boyfriend to give to Fai), Fai takes him in and nurses him. Tensions remain between the two of them. Fai leaves the bar and works in a Chinese restaurant, where coworker Chang (Chen) subtly flirts with him, although the two never take it to the next level. Fai returns to Hong Kong via Taipei, where he visits Chang's family's restaurant.

★ ★

One of today's most acclaimed directors, Wong Kar-Wai makes films that aren't so much about plot as they are about mood, music, color, and character. With films like *Chungking Express* (1994) and *In the Mood for Love* (2000), he weaves haunting and poignant portraits of love and the confusion and chaos it creates in unsuspecting people. Turning his gaze to a queer love story for the first time, he captures a similarly intimate sweep with these two characters who drive each other crazy and yet can't seem to stay apart. This is one of those movies where what isn't said is just as important as what is, and if you can let go of the idea of conventional storytelling, you'll get a lot out of this gorgeous film. (Watch for the subtle use of freeze frame and slow motion in the scene where Fai and Chang say goodbye—it speaks volumes about the unspoken and unconsummated attraction between the two of them.) If nothing else, luxuriate in the always-gorgeous cinematography of Wong's frequent collaborator Christopher Doyle, whose credits also include *Hero* (2002) and the Gus Van Sant remake of *Psycho* (1998).

Quotes to Remember:

> **Po:** Do you regret being with me?
> **Fai:** You bet I do! I had no regrets until I met you. Now my regrets could kill me!

HEATHERS

(1989)

Written by Daniel Waters.
Directed by Michael Lehmann.
Winona Ryder, Christian Slater, Shannen Doherty, Lisanne Falk,
Kim Walker, Patrick Labyorteaux, Lance Fenton.
(Anchor Bay Entertainment)

Veronica Sawyer (Ryder) becomes part of Westerberg High's most powerful clique, the Heathers, but finds that life is empty at the top of the teenage food chain. The new kid in school, Jason Dean (Slater), catches Veronica's fancy and goads her into helping him kill the popular kids and make their deaths look like suicides. Alpha girl Heather Chandler (Walker) is given a cup of poison, while hetero football jocks Kurt (Fenton) and Ram (Labyorteaux) are shot in such a way that suggests they were lovers who killed each other. Unfortunately, Ms. Chandler becomes revered in death, and the formerly quiet Heather Duke (Doherty) wants to take over as queen bee. Will Jason succeed in blowing up the entire school to make a statement, or can Veronica find other means to make everyone stop acting like such assholes?

★ ★

One of the most coal-black dark comedies ever made, *Heathers* dazzled audiences with its biting wit and striking visual style, not to mention the star-making performances from Ryder and Slater. (It's a pity that Walker, so exquisitely bitchy here, didn't get the career boost she so deserved from *Heathers* before her tragic death at 33 from a brain tumor in 2001.) Subsequent films, particularly 2004's *Mean Girls*, have tried to capture the same evil magic, but none have the same sting. And since it has often been observed that gay male society is often like high school—with petty gossip, rigid social castes based on looks and wealth, and empty pretty people strutting about like they own the joint—*Heathers* is the perfect tonic for anyone who's wanted to see the head cheerleader and football team captain get taken down a peg or two. Like *Carrie* (see p. 46), this film is clearly the kind of movie Hollywood could no longer make after the Columbine shooting, but *Heathers* remains a wonderfully nasty high school satire.

Quotes to Remember:

Heather Chandler: Fuck me gently with a chain saw. Do I look like Mother Theresa?

Jason: The extreme always seems to make an impression.

Veronica: No, my life's not perfect. I don't really like my friends.
Jason: Yeah, I don't really like your friends either.
Veronica: Well, it's just like...they're people I work with, and our job is being popular and shit.

Heather Duke (praying over the coffin of Heather Chandler): I prayed for the death of Heather Chandler many times. And I felt bad every time I did it, but I kept doing it anyway. Now I know you understood everything. Praise Jesus. Hallelujah!

Jason (explaining why he's leaving a bottle of mineral water with Kurt and Ram's fake suicide note): This is Ohio. If you don't have a brewski in your hand, you might as well be wearing a dress.

Girl: Did you hear? School's cancelled today because Kurt and Ram killed themselves in a repressed homosexual suicide pact. [beat]
Heather Duke: No way!

Kurt's dad (eulogizing): If there's any way you can hear me, Kurt buddy, I don't care that you really were some pansy. You're my own flesh and blood and, well, you made me proud. My son's a homosexual, and I love him. I love my dead gay son!
Jason (whispering to Veronica): I wonder how he'd feel if that limp wrist still had a pulse in it.

Veronica: My teen angst bullshit has a body count...Are we going to prom, or to hell?

See Also:

Probably the best of the post-*Heathers* high school comedies is *Election* (1999)—what it lacks in homicide, it makes up for in skullduggery, intrigue, and unabashed student-teacher hatred.

HEDWIG AND THE ANGRY INCH

(2001)

Written and directed by John Cameron Mitchell,
based on his musical play.
John Cameron Mitchell, Michael Pitt, Miriam Shor, Stephen Trask,
Andrea Martin. (New Line Home Video)

While performing a concert tour in a national chain of seafood restaurants, "internationally ignored song stylist" Hedwig (Mitchell) tells us her story: Born in East Germany, gay boy Hansel gets a sex-change operation to marry an American officer. But the botched surgery left Hedwig with neither penis nor vagina, just an "angry inch." Abandoned by her Army husband, Hedwig starts making music and falls in love with dorky teenager Tommy (Pitt), whom she teaches about rock and roll. Tommy—using the stage name Hedwig gave him, "Tommy Gnosis"—steals her songs and becomes a big success, but Hedwig—traveling with a backup band, a fast-talking manager (Martin), and embittered, gender-ambiguous spouse Yitzhak (Shor)—remains determined to reunite with the man she thinks of as her other half.

★ ★

John Cameron Mitchell (Hedwig) and Michael Pitt (Tommy)

As far as debut films from writer-director-stars go, *Hedwig and the Angry Inch* is right up there with *Citizen Kane* and *Take the Money and Run* (1969) in my book. (And this *is* my book, so there.) Mitchell's story takes a city divided in two (cold war–era Berlin) and examines gender split in two and the idea that all human souls are a half looking to make a whole. But once you get past the multiple metaphors, you've got very funny dialogue and terrific rock songs from Stephen Trask (formerly of the band Sugar). *Hedwig* will leave you humming the songs, quoting the lines, and maybe even changing the way you look at men, women, and the world. (You definitely won't be able to look at actress Rachel Griffiths again without thinking about how much she looks like John Cameron Mitchell in drag.)

Quotes to Remember:

Hedwig (talking to fans): Tommy, can you hear me? From this milkless tit you sucked the very business we call show. OK, you wanna know about Tommy Gnosis? After my divorce, I scraped by with baby-sitting gigs and odd jobs—mostly the jobs we call blow. I lost my job at the base PX, and I lost my gag reflex. You do the math.

Tommy: Have you accepted Jesus Christ as your personal lord and savior?
Hedwig: No, but I...I love his work.

Yitzhak (introducing Hedwig): On August 13, 1961, a wall was erected down the middle of the city of Berlin. The world was divided by a cold war, and the Berlin Wall was the most hated symbol of that divide. Reviled, graffiti'd, spit upon. We thought the wall would stand forever. And now that it's gone, we don't know who we are anymore. Ladies and gentlemen, Hedwig is like that wall, standing before you in a divide between East and West, slavery and freedom, man and woman, top and bottom.

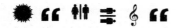

HENRY & JUNE

(1990)

Written by Philip Kaufman and Rose Kaufman,
from the book by Anaïs Nin.
Directed by Philip Kaufman.
Maria de Medeiros, Fred Ward, Richard E. Grant,
Uma Thurman, Kevin Spacey. (Universal Home Video)

Anaïs Nin (De Medeiros) lives in 1930s Paris with her husband, Hugo (Grant), working on her writing and keeping an extensive diary. She meets American author Henry Miller (Ward), whose brutish exterior and raw, sexual prose intrigue her. Henry has a tempestuous relationship with his wife, June (Thurman), whose relationship with a "patron" has helped to pay for Henry's writings. Nin becomes lovers with Henry, but also remains obsessed with June. With the input and inspiration of both women, Henry finishes *Tropic of Cancer*. And Nin writes about it all in her diaries, although the story of her relationship with the Millers wasn't published until the 1980s, after the three of them and Hugo had all died.

★ ★

Director Philip Kaufman's film isn't just a look at an interesting literary anecdote; it's one of the few films—particularly out of Hollywood—to examine a woman's sexuality and her right to explore and express it. On the surface, I realize it sounds like I'm describing *Emmanuelle* (1974) or a host of late-night Cinemax offerings, but *Henry & June* never feels like it's a man's interpretation of what excites and intrigues a woman. In capturing Nin's sexual awakening, Kaufman plunges into a world of raw sexuality where everything is possible. As gay as I am, I get a real charge out of this film, even the lesbian sequences. There's an amazing scene where Nin and her husband go to a bordello to watch two women have sex. One of the whores takes on the "male" role until Nin finally tells her "Stop pretending to be a man," which leads the two performers to truly make love to each other. It's hot stuff. Too bad that Kaufman's view of the Parisian demimonde features no shortage of lesbians but just one drag queen. (The ancestor of the one in *Glitter* [see p. 93], perhaps?)

HUSTLER WHITE

(1996)

Written and directed by Rick Castro and Bruce LaBruce.
Tony Ward, Bruce LaBruce, Alex Austin, Kevin Kramer, Ron Athey,
Glen Meadmore, Vaginal Davis. (Strand Releasing Home Video)

German writer Jürgen Anger (LaBruce) comes to Los Angeles to write about the sex trade and immediately becomes smitten with street hustler Monty Ward (Ward). As Anger pursues the object of his obsession, we encounter other denizens of this world, including a mortician (Athey) with a proclivity for drag, tattoos, and mummification, and a "trash twink" (Kramer) who "auditions" for a stable of hustlers of color.

★ ★

Sexy, silly, and outrageous, *Hustler White* is a brilliantly conceived comedy about rent boys and the odd ducks who hire them. Bracketed by references to *Sunset Blvd.* (see p. 202) and *What Ever Happened to Baby Jane?* (see p. 226), *Hustler White* takes us up and down Santa Monica Boulevard to hustler hangouts, seedy motel rooms, and some very scary places. Some of the sex scenes are definitely not for the squeamish—I'm just going to say "amputee fetish," and leave it at that—while others are played very much for laughs. (One of the black studs uses a Wonder Bread bag as a condom when fucking petite blond Kramer.) LaBruce gives one of his most assured performances as

Tony Ward (Montgomery) and Bruce LaBruce (Jürgen Anger)

the supercilious and Teutonic Anger, whose bitchy exterior melts away as he grows ever more besotted with Ward.

AUTEUR ALERT:

From his 8mm debut feature *No Skin Off My Ass* (1991) to his outrageous satires *Super 8-1/2* (1993) and *The Raspberry Reich* (2004), Canadian punk Bruce LaBruce is one of the rare queer filmmakers to combine explicit sexuality and political dogma. His movies are rough and occasionally disturbing, but always unpredictable, thought-provoking, and hot. See them.

I'VE HEARD THE MERMAIDS SINGING

(1987)

Written and directed by Patricia Rozema.
Sheila McCarthy, Paule Baillargeon, Ann-Marie MacDonald.
(Miramax Home Entertainment)

"Organizationally impaired" Polly (McCarthy) becomes "person Friday" to the cool and continental curator (Baillargeon) of a small Toronto gallery. An amateur photographer herself, Polly becomes smitten with "The Curator" (as Polly calls her) and her blithely intellectual knowledge about art. (The Curator tosses around phrases like "oblique pragmatism" and "flabby euphemisms" without batting a perfectly-styled eyelash.) When Polly discovers a roomful of extraordinary paintings by The Curator, Polly prevails upon her to display them, to much success. But The Curator's vicious appraisal of Polly's own photographs (submitted pseudonymously) sends Polly on a downward spiral, until she discovers...Well, you just have to see the movie.

★ ★

Rozema's acclaimed debut feature is a meditation on art and talent. It's also delightfully funny and so wonderfully oddball that it's the rare movie that's huggable without being gooey. McCarthy underplays perfectly as the awkward Polly—there's a Japanese restaurant sequence that's a little gem of physical and verbal comedy—but she also captures the character's sunny spirit and unpretentious creativity. The film takes its title from the poem "The Love Song of J. Alfred Prufrock," but by the end, we know that Polly, unlike T.S. Eliot's protagonist, will dare to eat a peach.

Quote to Remember:

> **Polly:** I think I kind of fell in love with The Curator. I know love is a pretty strong word when you're talking about another woman and she's not your mother, but there you go. I don't think I wanted kissing and all that stuff. I just...I just loved her.

Fun Facts:

★ To force the audience to envision The Curator's masterful paintings, Rozema never shows them to us; the paintings are nothing more than framed light. I remain convinced that Quentin Tarantino stole this idea for Ving Rhames's briefcase in *Pulp Fiction* (1994).

★ Anne-Marie McDonald, who plays The Curator's girlfriend, Mary Joseph, has gone on to become a novelist of note, whose works include *The Way the Crow Flies* and *Fall on Your Knees*.

★ The "Flower Duet" from the opera *Lakmé*, which is heard throughout the film, became quite popular in the 1980s, popping up in *The Hunger, Five Corners* (1987), and a British Airways ad.

JACKASS: THE MOVIE

(2002)

Directed by **Jeff Tremaine.**
Johnny Knoxville, Chris "Party Boy" Pontius, Steve-O,
Bam Margera, Ryan Dunn, Jason "Wee Man" Acuña, Preston Lacy,
Ehren McGhehey, Spike Jonze, Rip Taylor. (Paramount Home Video)

The skateboarders–stuntmen–thrill-seeking idiots of the MTV hit *Jackass* take their act to the big screen. Johnny Knoxville drives a rental car in a demolition derby, wearing a helmet with a big rainbow sticker on it. Chris Pontius turns on his "Party Boy" music, tears away a sweat suit to reveal a G-string and dances up to and rubs himself against unsuspecting citizens of Tokyo. Steve-O and Pontius pretend to masturbate underwater by rubbing sea cucumbers, which defend themselves by emitting a milky discharge. The boys attach muscle stimulators to the area between their ass and balls, which they refer to as "the gooch." Pontius puts on a bikini and rabbit ears and calls himself "Bunny the Lifeguard." Knoxville, covered in old-age makeup, pretends to be a very bad shoplifter—when he is kicked out of the store, he shouts, "I was Lon Chaney's lover!" Steve-O dangles over an alligator pit with a chicken leg hanging out of his butt. Steve-O shoots a bottle rock-

118

et, tied to Pontius's penis, out of his ass. Ryan Dunn shoves a toy car up his rectum and goes for an X-ray. And then Rip Taylor heaves confetti and tells us the movie is over.

★ ★

Lord, how gay can these boys get? Director John Waters has discussed his adoration for the "sexual anarchy" of *Jackass*, and this movie shows the cast's naughty fervor over and over again. There's something to be said for a new generation of dudes who romp around naked with each other without feeling the need to constantly proclaim their heterosexuality. (Quite the contrary, in fact—see Quote to Remember, below.) The *Jackass* guys are clearly comfortable with their sexuality, and they invite audiences of all stripes to enjoy their thong-clad silliness. Why is a little person in a panda costume falling off a skateboard in downtown Tokyo funny? I don't know; it just *is*. I can still vividly remember seeing *Jackass* in the theater and leaving with a sore throat because of the (1) laughing, (2) screaming, and (3) dry heaves during the "yellow sno-cone" sequence.

Quote to Remember:

[From the DVD outtakes]
Chris Pontius: Does Party Boy prefer men or women? He doesn't care. When the bear is hungry, he'll eat.

THE KILLING OF SISTER GEORGE

(1968)

Written by Lukas Heller,
based on the play by Frank Marcus.
Directed by Robert Aldrich.
Beryl Reid, Susannah York, Coral Browne. (MGM Home Entertainment)

June (Reid) is a boozy actress of a certain age, playing kindly country nurse Sister George on a BBC soap opera and living with Childie (York), her lover. The two have a relationship that balances between the amorous and the contentious, with some minor dominance-submission games thrown in for good measure. Network executive Mercy (Browne—who, in real life, was Vincent Price's co-beard) tries to warn June that her days on the soap may be numbered, but Mercy winds up seducing Childie and taking her away.

★ ★

Made in an era when movies about queers tended to be exploitative freak shows or movies about the "homosexual problem," *The Killing of Sister George* is fascinating in that it's not lesbianism per se on which the plot turns. When June's job is in trouble, it's not because she's a big dyke—it's because she drinks too much and says the wrong thing (often something hilarious that scandalizes her uptight listeners) and throws tantrums and molests nuns in taxicabs. The central love triangle features no victims, just victimizers who have been out-strategized. As with Aldrich and Heller's *What Ever Happened to Baby Jane?* (see p. 226), it's best not to make assumptions too quickly as to who is the wronged party and who is manipulating whom. Lest gay men feel they hold a patent on drama and head games, here's a movie that reminds us that our lesbian sisters are no slouches in that department themselves. (And get a load of those Coral Browne dragon-lady-via-*Ladies' Home Journal* outfits!)

Quotes to Remember:

Childie: Not all girls are bloody raving lesbians, you know.
June: That is a misfortune that I am perfectly well aware of.

June (to Childie): But since what you know about poetry wouldn't cover one tile in a public lavatory, it's reasonable to suppose that Mrs. Mercy Bloody Croft's overpowering interest in you is other than poetic!

See Also:

The wonderfully terrible *The Legend of Lylah Clare* (1968), the third of what might be called Aldrich's "actress trilogy," also featuring Browne. Kim Novak plays a reincarnated screen diva and camps it up madly. Hee-larious.

KINSEY

(2004)

Written and directed by Bill Condon.
Liam Neeson, Laura Linney, Peter Sarsgaard, Chris O'Donnell,
Tim Curry, John Lithgow, Lynn Redgrave.
(Twentieth Century Fox Home Entertainment)

Alfred Kinsey (Neeson), a leading entomologist, comes to realize soon after his marriage to Clara (Linney) that there is very limited scientific knowledge about human sexuality. In an attempt to exhaustively study human behavior in the way that he had once studied the gall wasp, Kinsey begins a thorough survey of sex behavior, realizing that no one can state what is "normal" without knowing what it is that people actually do. He overcomes American fear and prejudices and has a big hit with his 1948 study, *Sexual Behavior in the Human Male*. Along the way he learns a thing or two about his own sexuality, having his first same-sex affair with research assistant Clyde Martin (Sarsgaard), who later sleeps with Clara. But Kinsey's companion volume about female sexuality, published during the conservative McCarthy era of the 1950s, attracts detractors and scorn. Through it all, Kinsey pushes on in his struggle to save Americans from sexual ignorance.

★ ★

One of the screen's smartest—and certainly sexiest—biopics, Bill Condon's *Kinsey* explores the fascinating life of a man who completely changed American culture by bringing sexual taboos out of the closet where they could be, if not always accepted, at least openly discussed. What's so fascinating about the movie is that it simultaneously operates on so many levels. You have the story of a scientist trying to catalogue human behavior and learning that such methodology may work up to a point—it's a lot trickier to quantify love in a scientific setting than it is to discuss sex. At the same time, *Kinsey* reminds us of the cyclical nature of history—while Kinsey and his discoveries no doubt helped set into motion the sexual revolution of the 1960s and '70s, the film itself was released around the time of George W. Bush's reelection, when abstinence education had somehow wormed its way back into the curriculum and conservatives were talking about same-sex marriage like it was the apocalypse. For all its big ideas, however, *Kinsey* is ultimately an intimate story of a man's life, and it succeeds beautifully on that level. Neeson is brilliant in the lead role, and the delicate dance of seduction that he and Sarsgaard perform around each other is a real treat.

Quotes to Remember:

Kinsey (reading a 1930s "marriage guide"): It's all just hooey. Morality disguised as fact.

Interviewee: It's not that I mind being queer. 'Cause I don't. It's just, um...I wish other folks weren't so put out by it.
Kinsey: Homosexuality happens to be out of fashion in society now. That doesn't mean it won't change someday.
Interviewee: Right. [Ruefully chuckles]

Clyde: This rating scale of yours?
Kinsey: Mm-hmm?
Clyde: Uh, zero to six...
Kinsey: Zero being exclusively heterosexual and, uh, six being exclusively homosexual. A great many people line up somewhere

in the middle.

Clyde: What makes you think that's true?

Kinsey: Common sense. Remember, about a third of our hetero-sexual histories have homosexual acts, and vice versa.

Clyde: Right. I guess I'm about a three, huh?

Kinsey: Based on your sexual history, I'd say that's, um, right.

Clyde: How about you?

Kinsey: I suppose I've been a one or two most of my life, even though it's taken a long time to recognize it.

Clyde: And now?

Kinsey: Probably th-three.

Clyde: Have you ever done anything about it? [Kinsey looks down] Would you like to? [They kiss]

Kinsey: The enforcers of chastity are massing once again, to dis-suade the scientist, intimidate him, convince him to cease research!

THE LAST OF SHEILA

(1973)

Written by Anthony Perkins and Stephen Sondheim.
Directed by Herbert Ross.
James Coburn, Richard Benjamin,
Joan Hackett, Dyan Cannon, James Mason, Raquel Welch,
Ian McShane. (Warner Home Video)

One year after the hit-and-run death of his beloved wife, Sheila, producer Clinton (Coburn) hosts a yacht party on the Riviera, inviting people with two things in common: They all desperately need work from Clinton, and they were all at the party at his house the night Sheila died. Clinton engages everyone in a party game in which everyone has to try to guess the "secrets" that the other guests have been assigned in an envelope. But wouldn't you know it, all the secrets ("I am a homosexual," "I am an ex-convict," etc.) are real-life skeletons in his guests' closets. Soon, plots are unraveling within plots, leading to a deliciously intricate web of intrigue in which everyone seems guilty and everything (including the film's title) becomes a clue in the script's Chinese box of games, paying testament to the puzzle mania of gay screenwriters Perkins (yes, the actor) and Sondheim (yes, the composer).

★ ★

A guilty gay secret, Hollywood lushes, Dyan Cannon as a loudmouth Sue Mengers-ish agent, gossip, deception, and a closing song by Bette Midler. How 1973 gay can you get? What's most fun about this triple-acrostic of a movie is that it's easy to forget all the whodunit explanations between viewings. While the costumes (by Joel Schumacher, who would later become a director and even later come out of the closet) and the cheesy score sometimes make the movie seem like an all-star episode of *The NBC Mystery Movie*, *Sheila* holds up as a cynical and hilarious send-up of Hollywood backstabbery.

See Also:

> *Sleuth* (1972), whose audience-befuddling complexity and gay subtext make this the perfect double feature, not to mention the fact that the working title of Anthony Shaffer's original play was *Who's Afraid of Stephen Sondheim?*

THE LIVING END

(1992)

Written and directed by Gregg Araki.
Mike Dytri, Craig Gilmore, Darcy Marta,
Mary Woronov, Johanna Went. (VHS only; Fox Lorber Home Video)

Film critic Jon (Gilmore) has just been diagnosed as HIV-positive. Hustler Luke (Dytri), who's already seroconverted, may have just killed a cop. Driven by passion and nihilism, they hit the road. Has Jon gotten in over his head? How loose a cannon is Luke? These lovers on the run will discover a lot about each other before their journey is done.

★ ★

Inspired by legendary French filmmaker Jean-Luc Godard—who was in turn inspired by Hollywood gangster pictures of the '30s and '40s—Araki's *amour fou* epic divided queer audiences and remains one of the most vivid and sexy gay indie movies ever made. Marrying the righteous indignation of ACT UP with the fuck-the-world aesthetic of punk rock, Araki's grainy, no-budget road epic gave voice to the first wave of survivors of the AIDS pandemic. His heroes weren't going to take their HIV diagnosis lying down, even if their talk of going after Bush and injecting him with their blood was nothing but bluster. After a decade of safer-sex messages, it was exhilarating to see two attractive screen heroes driven by raw, animal passion in this "irresponsible" movie. Like most lovers-on-the-run sagas, *The Living End* isn't always quite sure where to go after that first burst of adrenaline wears off, but the movie remains fascinating both as a snapshot of a specific era and as a love story that could seemingly go off in any direction at any time.

Quotes to Remember:

Doctor (giving Jon test results, in the driest deadpan possible): Positive. Sorry.

Luke: We're victims of the sexual revolution. The generation before us had all the fun, and we get to pick up the fucking tab. Anybody who got fucked before safe sex...*is* fucked.

Jon: All I know is that if I don't take a shower and brush my teeth in like two minutes, I'm gonna kill myself. I'm a fag, OK? I can't stand being dirty.

Jon (driving the car): I'm not going to fondle your crotch right now.
Luke: Why not?
Jon: Because I'm a responsible driver.

Fun facts:

★ The film's heroes, Jon and Luke, are so named in homage to Jean-Luc Godard, an idol of Araki's. Jon's apartment has posters from Godard's *Made in U.S.A.* (1966) and *Nouvelle Vague* (1990).

Craig Gilmore (Jon) and Mike Dytri (Luke)

★ Producer Jon Gerrans has a cameo as one of the three gay-bashers who encounter Luke. Gerrans (who's straight) and fellow producer Marcus Hu (who isn't) are copresidents of Strand Releasing, a mainstay of queer independent cinema. At the time the film was being made, Hu was working for another film distribution company and snuck in after hours to photocopy scripts and steal supplies for the set.

★ Noted queer director Christopher Münch (*The Hours and Times, The Sleepy Time Gal*) did the film's lighting.

★ Because of the film's low budget, it was shot entirely in Southern California, even though Jon and Luke are supposedly traveling through several states. Araki got the footage of Texas highway signs from Austin-based director Richard Linklater.

AUTEUR ALERT:

After bursting onto the scene with *The Living End*, Gregg Araki has continually kept audiences and critics on their toes with a series of bold, sexy, and anarchic films. From his "Teen Apocalypse" trilogy of *Totally F***ed Up* (1993), *The Doom Generation* (1995), and *Nowhere* (1997) to his new-wave-Noel-Coward screwball comedy *Splendor* (1999) to his acclaimed adaptation of Scott Heim's *Mysterious Skin* (2005), Araki's films are occasionally infuriating but always nervy, bold, and memorable.

THE LONELY LADY

(1983)

Written by John Kershaw and Shawn Randall;
adaptation by Ellen Shepard, from the novel by Harold Robbins.
Directed by Peter Sasdy.
Pia Zadora, Lloyd Bochner, Bibi Besch, Joseph Cali,
Anthony Holland, Jared Martin, Ray Liotta.
(VHS only; Universal Home Video)

As she arrives at "the Awards" (this isn't a script that gets bogged down in specifics), writer Jerilee Randall (Zadora) reflects on how she got there. After winning a writing prize at Valley High, teenage Jerilee winds up at a Beverly Hills party where a boy (Liotta) rapes her with a garden hose. Later, she is comforted by the owner of the house, acclaimed screenwriter Walter Thornton (Bochner). The two marry, even though he is much older. They have sexual problems, and Walter takes credit for a rewrite Jerilee does to his movie. (The rewrite comprises of taking out a grieving mother's soliloquy and replacing it with "WHY???") On her own, she struggles to sell her script. She has an affair with married actor George Ballantine (Martin) who doesn't even bother to accompany her when she goes to abort his child. A sleazy club owner (Cali) promises to back her screenplay but just uses her for sex. Jerilee has a nervous breakdown and then writes a script about everything that has happened to her. For the movie to be made, she has to agree to let George be the star, and she has to take a dip in a hot tub with the financier's wife. When she wins "the Award," she shocks the crowd by saying she's not the only person who's had to fuck her way to the top.

★ ★

There are some movies so bad that even the props are all wrong, and this is one of them. (Just look at the clunky microphones used by the TV guy in the very first scene. It's an omen of what's to come.) This utterly bugfuck showbiz epic features ridiculous dialogue ("If I write for anyone, I write for *m-e-e-e!*"), hideous acting from Zadora on down, and oh, that garden hose rape scene. Not only is the scene itself a howler—I know, rape's not funny, but you just have to see this one for yourself—but later in the movie, disgruntled husband Walter waves the very same hose in her face and bellows, "Or maybe *this* is more your kick?" (Wouldn't he have switched to sprinklers?) Pia Zadora owed her film career to a very rich and ambitious husband, Meshulam Riklis, who thought this would be a good vehicle for her; decades later on Zadora's *E! True Hollywood Story*, her husband noted, "Look, don't blame *me* for everything." Did I mention how embarrassed Bochner looks to be kissing Zadora? Or the fact that her nervous breakdown scene has the faces of those who've wronged her flying out of her typewriter after she takes a shower fully clothed? Or that Rome, Italy, unconvincingly stands in for Hollywood, U.S.A.? You won't believe that anyone sat down and wrote this thing, much less shot, edited, and distributed it. Get your friends together and have a good laugh at *The Lonely Lady*.

Pia Zadora (Jerilee)

Quotes to Remember:

[Jerilee and Walter have just encountered a clingy, needy actress asking Walter for a job]

Jerilee: Walter, who would want to be an actress?

Walter: In this business, you can't afford self-respect.

Producer (telling Jerilee she has to agree to let George star in her movie): You've already had one abortion; don't make it two.

Jerilee: Same father.

MAHOGANY

(1975)

Written by John Byrum,
from a story by Toni Amber.
Directed by Berry Gordy.
Diana Ross, Billy Dee Williams, Anthony Perkins,
Jean-Pierre Aumont. (VHS only; Paramount Home Entertainment)

Tracy Chambers (Ross) is an ambitious would-be fashion designer, hoping to make her way out of Chicago's ghetto. She falls in love with rising young politician Brian (Williams) but leaves him behind when she has the chance to go to Rome to be a fashion model for famous photographer Sean (Perkins), who rechristens her "Mahogany." She becomes a top supermodel and eventually gets to design her own collection, but she realizes that Brian was right when he told her, "Success means nothing without someone you love to share it with."

★ ★

Bro-*ther*! A movie like *Mahogany* raises many more questions than it could ever answer. How did they get away with making a prefeminist movie, where a woman ditches her career for her man, in the middle of the '70s? Is Diana Ross intentionally doing a bad job of playing a high-strung diva in the hopes that we'll believe that it's not her natural state? What possessed Diana to design—much less take credit for—the ludicrous fashions in this movie? Who let Motown executive Berry Gordy behind a camera after the first two directors fell by the wayside?

And most importantly, did anyone try to retract Diana's Oscar nomination for *Lady Sings the Blues* (1972) after this movie came out? Besides its camp value, *Mahogany* does provide some lasting value to gay audiences. For one thing, you get to see gay actor Perkins slither around like the honky villain of a blaxploitation movie. There's also a glimpse of comedian Bruce Vilanch, still in his baby-bear phase. And perhaps most importantly, Diana's big fashion-model montage—which is even crazier than the Gillian Girl TV commercial in *Valley of the Dolls* (see p. 216)—plays like the template for every look RuPaul has ever tried.

MAKING LOVE

(1982)

Written by Barry Sandler;
story by A. Scott Berg.
Directed by Arthur Hiller.
Michael Ontkean, Kate Jackson, Harry Hamlin,
Wendy Hiller, Arthur Hill.
(VHS only—can you imagine?
Twentieth Century Fox Home Entertainment)

Zach (Ontkean), a doctor, is seemingly happily married to network executive Claire (Jackson). Zach suddenly finds himself hanging out in gay bars and at gay cruising spots, but he doesn't connect with anyone. He becomes friends with Bart (Hamlin), a gay author who's commitment-phobic. Zach and Bart go to bed, but it's clear that Bart isn't looking for a relationship. Zach tells Claire he is gay; she is devastated. Zach moves away so they can both start over. They reconnect a few years later at a funeral, and both are in love with new men.

★ ★

It's easy to mock *Making Love* for Harry Hamlin's *Moment by Moment* (see p. 145) hair or for its goody-two-shoes protagonists—He works with cancer patients! She's fighting for quality television!—but this movie was genuinely revolutionary at the time of its release, and it remains a lot bolder than Hollywood's subsequent efforts at dealing with the lives and loves of gay peo-

Michael Ontkean (background, as Zach) and Harry Hamlin (Bart)

ple. For one thing, Hamlin and Ontkean actually kiss, which is more than Oscar-winner Tom Hanks did with Antonio Banderas in *Philadelphia*. Besides the film's relative openness about same-sex physicality, it also provides a compassionate and multi-dimensional portrait of gay men. With Reagan in office and the first panicky years of the AIDS pandemic, the '80s would not see another movie this smart and this well-made about gay issues except from independent or foreign filmmakers. Some may dismiss the film as a "pretty white people with problems" movie, but I watched *Making Love* in a packed theater for the film's 20th anniversary and was struck with how resonant and interesting it still is. And as long as married men continue to reach the realization that they're gay, there will always be people to whom this film speaks with direct frankness.

Quotes to Remember:

Zach (to Bart): It's not as if I'm gay. I'm just...curious.

Claire: I thought I knew you. Who are you?
Zach: I'm the man who's loved you for eight years.
Claire: Loved me or used me? You used me, you hid behind me for eight years!

Fun fact:

★ A. Scott Berg, who received a story credit, was the boyfriend of screenwriter Sandler when this film was made. Berg has gone on to greater fame for his biographies of Katharine Hepburn, Charles Lindbergh, and Sam Goldwyn, among others.

MANJI

(1964)

Written by Kaneto Shindô,
based on the novel by Junichirô Tanizaki.
Directed by Yasuzo Masumura.
Ayako Wakao, Kyôko Kishida, Yusuke Kawazu, Eiji Funakoshi.
(Fantoma Home Video)

Housewife Sonoko (Kishida) becomes smitten with young Mitsuko (Wakao), her classmate at an "art school for ladies." Their eventual relationship is complicated by Mitsuko's obsessive fiancé, Watanuki (Kawazu), and by Sonoko's husband, Kotaro (Funakoshi), who also becomes obsessed with the enigmatic and manipulative Mitsuko. Alliances are formed and broken. Things end badly.

★ ★

This tale of love and obsession may, in certain cultures, play like straightforward melodrama, but in the eyes of every audience with whom I've watched *Manji*, this film falls into a very rare category: Lesbian Camp. The overwrought emotions ("Kill me!" gets uttered by practically every character on at least one occasion), the blood oaths, the suicide pacts, the early-'60s hair and makeup, and the almost-but-not-quite graphic nudity combine to make this movie something of an exquisite laugh riot.

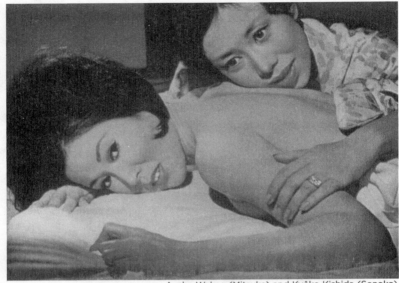

Ayako Wakao (Mitsuko) and Kyôko Kishida (Sonoko)

Quotes to Remember:

Sonoko (to Kotaro): You don't love me enough! I need more love!

[After Mitsuko first disrobes for Sonoko and wraps herself in a sheet]
Sonoko: It's too much! It's too much!
Mitsuko: What's happened to you?
Sonoko: When I see something beautiful, I become so excited I cry.
Mitsuko: Satisfied? Now I'll get dressed.
Sonoko: No! No! I want to see more.
Mitsuko: Silly! There's no point in keeping this up.
Sonoko: Yes there is! You're not completely nude. Take it off!

Sonoko (to Kotaro): Love between women is like love of a work of art.

Kotaro (to Sonoko): Even between women, being naked in broad daylight is not natural.

Mitsuko: I prefer women to like me much more than men. It's natural for men to think a woman pretty. But I attract women to me.

MAURICE

(1987)

Written by Kit Hesketh-Harvey and James Ivory,
from the novel by E.M. Forster.
Directed by James Ivory.
James Wilby, Hugh Grant, Rupert Graves, Billie Whitelaw, Ben
Kingsley, Helena Bonham-Carter. (Home Vision Entertainment)

While in college at Cambridge, Maurice Hall (Wilby) falls in love with aristocrat Clive Durham (Grant). While the feeling is mutual, Durham says that any relationship between two men must be platonic. Durham gets married, although he and Maurice remain friends. Maurice sees a hypnotist (Kingsley) to be cured of homosexuality, to no avail. On a visit to Clive's estate, Maurice meets the under-gameskeeper, Scudder (Graves); Scudder climbs a ladder into Maurice's room one night, and they make love. While Maurice is afraid that Scudder will blackmail him, the servant professes his love. The two make a go at being together, even though Edwardian society will not approve.

★ ★

Based on a posthumously published E.M. Forster novel, *Maurice* is something of a fantasia in which a gay upper-class twit can find true love with a servant in the most caste-conscious society this side of India. Still, if you can suspend disbelief enough, *Maurice* is a real treat, especially for people who like their gay films to be queer versions of straight movies. This one's yet another Forster adaptation from out filmmakers James

James Wilby (Maurice) and Hugh Grant (Clive)

Ivory and the late Ismail Merchant—who also made *A Room With a View* (1985) and *Howards End* (1992)—only this time, among the cricket flannels, sitting rooms, and high teas, we get hot dudes kissing and even some frontal nudity. Bring on the all-male *Lady Chatterley's Lover* next, I say.

Fun facts:

★ Helena Bonham-Carter's cameo here makes her three-for-three on the Merchant Ivory adaptations of Forster; she starred in *A Room With a View* and played a supporting role in *Howards End*.

★ A Los Angeles queer punk rock, film, and performance art festival called Scutterfest was named for the Scudder character in *Maurice*.

Quotes to Remember:

Hypnotist: I needn't remind you that your sort were once put to death in England. I would advise you to live in some country—France, Italy—where homosexuality is no longer criminal.
Maurice: Will it ever be like that in England?
Hypnotist: England has always been disinclined to accept human nature.

Maurice: I'm in love with Alec Scudder.
Clive: What a grotesque announcement.

MOMENT BY MOMENT

(1978)

Written and directed by Jane Wagner.
Lily Tomlin, John Travolta, Andra Akers.
(Not available on home video—write Universal a letter)

Estranged from her husband, Beverly Hills society matron Trisha (Tomlin) unsuccessfully attempts to pick up some sleeping pills on her way out to her Malibu beach house. Young street hustler Strip (Travolta) follows her out of the drugstore and tells her that he once worked as a valet parker at one of her parties. When Trisha arrives on the beach in Malibu, Strip appears again. While his persistence puts her off at first, the two become friends and, eventually, lovers. But can their affair survive their difference in age and social station?

★ ★

I got to interview Lily Tomlin once, and I couldn't *not* bring up *Moment by Moment*; she was amused when I told her that the infamous bomb would have done better had they done the entire thing in French. And I stand by that—1978 audiences giggled at this malaise-packed June-November romance, but I suspect that critics and moviegoers alike would have taken this languorous movie more seriously had it starred, say, Catherine

Deneuve and some shirtless Gallic stud. The movie does make
its share of mistakes, starting with having a character named
"Strip"; I couldn't help giggling during the infamous hot tub
scene Tomlin's character keeps saying "Strip" to a naked man.
And what's presented as Travolta's wooing of Tomlin often plays
more like stalking. It also doesn't help that Tomlin and Travolta,
in the words of one critic, look more alike than anyone in
Hollywood except maybe Lee Marvin and James Coburn. But
I'm endlessly fascinated by the fact that Tomlin's longtime
romantic and artistic partner, Jane Wagner, wrote and directed
this film, particularly since gay male writers and directors have
been churning out hetero romantic comedies and dramas in
Hollywood for decades. The way that Travolta's body is filmed in
a way that makes him an object of desire, the way that his character is the one who wants commitment, who wants to hear "I
love you"—this is the sort of thing you only get when there's a
woman behind the camera, be she straight, lesbian, or otherwise.
While it's no triumph, *Moment by Moment* is a rare movie that
actually tries to make a point about class and social status in
the United States. And Tomlin proves once again that she's a
capable dramatic actress on top of being a world-class comic. The
film skates back and forth between relevance and disaster, but
it's an interesting ride.

MOMMIE DEAREST

(1981)

**Written by Frank Yablans, Frank Perry,
Tracy Hotchner, and Robert Getchell,**
based on the book by Christina Crawford.
Directed by Frank Perry.
Faye Dunaway, Diana Scarwid, Mara Hobel,
Steve Forrest, Rutanya Alda. (Paramount Home Entertainment)

Movie star Joan Crawford (Dunaway) has a thriving career and an attentive lover, Greg (Forrest), but she wants a baby. She adopts little Christina. As the child (Hobel in childhood, Scarwid as adolescent and adult Tina) grows, Joan's behavior becomes more erratic. The actress tries to instill a competitive spirit in the child by beating her in swim races in their pool leaving Tina exhausted and half-drowned. When Joan catches Tina mimicking her, she hacks off the girl's hair and makes Tina's dolls (her "babies") disappear, in a not-so-subtle lesson about what happens to unruly children. On a rampage one night, Joan beats Tina for having a wire hanger in her closet and for not cleaning her bathroom well enough. Joan gets fired from MGM and destroys the rose garden in the middle of the night. Teenage Tina is sent off to boarding school and then later a convent school. Tina becomes an actress in New York, eventually appearing on a soap opera; when she falls ill, her much older mother takes over the role of a young bride-to-be. Joan eventually dies, leaving Tina and her brother

Christopher nothing in the will. Tina decides that Joan won't have the last word.

★ ★

Accept no imitations: *Mommie Dearest* is one of the flat-out craziest movies ever made. Child abuse is by no means funny, but—like the rape in *The Lonely Lady* (see p. 131)—incompetent movies have a way of turning horrible tragedy into gut-busting comedy without intending to do so. At the center of this maelstrom is Dunaway, whose portrayal of Crawford is mostly ludicrous, from her drag-queen eyebrows to her sumo-wrestler stance. She bellows out lines like *"Tina!* Bring me the ax!" and "I don't ask for much from you, *girl!*" and it's just the damnedest thing you ever saw. Apologists say that her performance merely mirrors Crawford's onscreen work in films like *Harriet Craig* (1950) and *Strait-Jacket* (1964), but little touches like crossing her eyes at the climax of the immortal "no wire hangers" scene make Dunaway go way, *way* past anything Crawford ever did. The oft-abused word *camp* applies when a movie that was intended to be serious and dramatic winds up hilarious and ridiculous. You can't set out to make camp—a film can be intentionally over-the-top, but that's a whole 'nother thing. Camp can only be created by mistake. *Mommie Dearest* is as camp as they come.

MY OWN PRIVATE IDAHO

(1991)

Written and directed by Gus Van Sant.
River Phoenix, Keanu Reeves, James Russo, William Richert,
Chiara Caselli, Flea, Mickey Cottrell. (Criterion Collection)

Mike Waters (Phoenix) is a narcoleptic street hustler looking to be reunited with his long-lost mother. His best friend on the streets is another hustler, Scott Favor (Reeves), the wastrel son of the mayor. Scott's many friends, including small-time crook Bob (Richert), hope that Scott will take care of them when he comes into his inheritance. Mike and Scott travel to Idaho and then to Italy to find Mike's mother. Scott falls in love with an Italian girl (Caselli) and, following the death of his father, steps into his rightful role as heir, turning his back on his former friends. Mike falls asleep on a stretch of highway in Idaho.

★ ★

A distinctive mix of John Rechy-esque hustling tales and Shakespeare's *Henry IV* (with Scott standing in for the slumming Prince Hal and Bob as his Falstaff), *My Own Private Idaho* signaled a new era for queer independent cinema. Not only did it boast the distinct visual style that made gay writer-director Van

Sant a star filmmaker following his first feature, *Drugstore Cowboy* (1989), but it also starred two of Hollywood's hottest young stars as rent boys. Early in the film, we see gay hustler Mike getting a blowjob from a john, and just as he's about to climax, Van Sant cuts to a house falling out of the sky and collapsing on a prairie road. That's the aesthetic at play here, and it works brilliantly. Even as Shakespearean argot starts spilling out of the mouths of street kids, Van Sant has created this world compellingly enough so that it all makes sense. It's a haunting and beautiful film.

Quotes to Remember:

> **Bob:** What time is it?
> **Scott:** What do you care? Why, you wouldn't even look at a clock unless hours were lines of coke, dials looked like the signs of gay bars, or time itself was a fair hustler in black leather.

> **Mike:** What do I mean to you?
> **Scott:** What do you mean to me? Mike, you're my best friend.
> **Mike:** I know, man. And I...I know I'm your friend. We're good friends. And it's good to be, you know, good friends. That's a good thing.
> **Scott:** So?
> **Mike:** So I just... [Scott sighs] That's OK. We can be friends.
> **Scott:** I only have sex with a guy for money.
> **Mike:** Yeah, I know.
> **Scott:** And two guys can't love each other.
> **Mike:** Yeah. Well, I don't know. I mean—I mean, for me—I could love someone even if I, you know, wasn't paid for it. I love you, and you don't pay me.

See Also:

> I can't really give Van Sant an AUTEUR ALERT on the off chance

that someone might accidentally wind up watching *Even Cowgirls Get the Blues* (1993) or *Last Days* (2005) or his version of *Psycho*. But you should totally check out *Drugstore Cowboy, Elephant* (2003), and, if you get the chance, his unavailable-on-video debut feature *Mala Noche* (1985). His biggest commercial hit, *Good Will Hunting* (1997), has an additional bonus for queer audiences in the loving way that Van Sant photographs Matt Damon and the brothers Affleck. It's like the adoring vision of Alain Delon in Luchino Visconti's *Rocco and His Brothers* (1960).

Aa

MYRA BRECKINRIDGE

(1970)

Written by David Giler and Michael Sarne,
from the novel by Gore Vidal.
Directed by Michael Sarne.
Raquel Welch, John Huston, Rex Reed, Mae West, Farrah Fawcett,
Roger Herren. (Twentieth Century Fox Home Entertainment)

Myron Breckinridge (Reed) has a sex-change operation and becomes Myra (Welch), although Myron does stick around to comment on the proceedings. Myra travels to Hollywood, where Myron's uncle, former cowboy star Buck Loner (Huston), runs a dramatic academy on land to which Myron's mother was entitled to half. Hoping to stall Myra (posing as Myron's widow) and her quest for the inheritance, Buck installs her at the school as a professor of posture and empathy. Myra is on a quest to eliminate traditional masculinity in an attempt to realign the sexes, so she sets her destructive sights on he-man Rusty (Herren)—who thinks that a man "ought to ball chicks"—and his girlfriend, Mary Ann (Fawcett). As Myron falls for Mary Ann and attempts to kill Myra, he awakens from the hallucination he suffered after having a car accident.

★ ★

Novelist Vidal—and pretty much the rest of the known world—despised *Myra Breckinridge* on its initial arrival into theaters, but the ensuing decades have been kind to this Hollywood satire. What was once seen as smutty and unfocused has emerged as a very smart and very ahead-of-its-time satire covering gender, movies, deconstructionism, and sex. Granted, the Mae West segments remain ridiculous—watching the 76-year-old starlet put the make on Tom Selleck and a parade of other young studs is, at best, baffling—but overall *Myra* plays a lot better for 21st-century audiences than for 1970 crowds. Of particular interest on the DVD is Sarne's director's cut: The longer scenes and restored transitions actually make big chunks of the movie make a great deal more sense. Current audiences may think of Rex Reed as an irrelevant film critic, but at the time of *Myra*, he was one of Hollywood's hottest cultural observers. If you can track down any of his very funny books of essays from this period, give him a read. And while Welch, in other films, isn't always as compelling a screen presence as one would like her to be, she really sinks her teeth into this trans-gender character, aided greatly by Theadora Van Runkle's 1940s-themed drag queen outfits.

THE OPPOSITE OF SEX

(1998)

Written and directed by Don Roos.
Christina Ricci, Martin Donovan, Lisa Kudrow, Lyle Lovett,
Ivan Sergei, Johnny Galecki. (Sony Pictures Home Entertainment)

After her stepfather dies, Dede (Ricci) leaves her home in Louisiana to visit her gay half-brother Bill (Donovan), a teacher. In short order, she seduces Bill's boyfriend, Matt (Sergei), and claims to be pregnant by him, and the two run off with the ashes of Bill's late partner, Tom. Bill, accompanied by Tom's shrewish sister Lucia (Kudrow), chase them to Los Angeles just after Matt's secret lover, Jason (Galecki), surfaces and threatens to tell the authorities that Bill molested Jason when they were student and teacher. And then things get *really* complicated...

★ ★

Don Roos was a successful Hollywood screenwriter with the scripts of *Boys on the Side* (1995) and *Single White Female* (1992) under his belt when he rocked the indie world with the pitch-black comedy *The Opposite of Sex*. Ricci's deadpan narration, featuring some of the most evil one-liners ever written (see below), made audiences both drop their jaws and convulse with laughter. It's appalling and appallingly funny, and the characters are all deliciously mordant. If you have a wicked sense of humor, *The Opposite of Sex* is one of those litmus-test movies you can show to potential boyfriends; if they don't laugh, kick 'em to the curb.

Quotes to Remember:

Dede (narrating): My mother was the kind of mother who always said she was her daughter's best friend. Whenever she did, I thought, *Great, not only do I have a shitty mother, but my best friend's a loser bitch.*

Dede (narrating, looking at Tom's ashes): Gross. But look at how pretty the urn is. That's typical gay.

Matt (after announcing he has slept with Dede): For your information, I'm bisexual.
Lucia: Please! I went to a bar mitzvah *once*. It doesn't make me Jewish. Who says that bisexual shit besides gay men?

Dede (narrating, about Jason): After high school he went to Chicago and became one of those ACT UP people who think AIDS is this big conspiracy against homos. Maybe it is, who knows? All I know is, it isn't working. There seem to be more of them than ever before, you know what I mean?

Lucia: Did you call that lawyer I told you about?
Bill: What for?
Lucia: Hello, this is America. We don't like sodomy so much here.
Bill: Yeah, but the schools are good.

Lucia: You've got a death wish. It's so selfish. I have one too, but

I direct it towards others.

Bill (to Jason): Listen to me, you little grunge faggot. I survived my family, my schoolyard, every Republican, every other Democrat, Anita Bryant, the pope, the fucking Christian Coalition, not to mention a real son of a bitch of a virus, in case you haven't noticed, and in all that time since Paul Lynde and Truman Capote were the only fairies in America, I've been busting my ass so that you'd be able to do what you wanted with yours! So I don't just want your obedience right now, which I do want and plenty of it, but I want your fucking gratitude, and I want it right fucking now, or you're going to be looking down a long road at your nipple in the dirt! Do you hear what I'm saying?

PARIS
IS
BURNING

(1990)

Directed by Jennie Livingston.
Willi Ninja, Pepper LaBeija, Dorian Corey, Freddie Pendavis,
Venus Xtravaganza. (Miramax Home Entertainment)

Shot in the pre-Giuliani New York City of 1987 and 1989, lesbian director Livingston's lively, funny, and occasionally poignant documentary examines the drag balls where black gay men compete. These pageants include not only the usual cross-dressing categories but also sections where competitors strive for "executive realness" (looking like a Wall Street type) or "banjee" (street thug). While these indefatigable and creative characters try to eke out an existence for themselves in a landscape of AIDS and poverty, the balls allow them to participate in the conspicuous consumption of the 1980s by doing their best imitation of the opulence they see around them and in the media. And in creating rival "houses," they create surrogate families for people who don't have one.

★ ★

Quotes to Remember:

Pepper Labeija: These balls are more or less our fantasy of being, like, a superstar. Like the Oscars or whatever. Or being on the runway as a model. A lot of these kids that are in the balls, they don't have two of nothing. Some of them don't even eat. They come to balls starving. And they sleep on the pier, whatever. They don't have a home to go to. They'll go out and steal something and get dolled up and come to a ball that one night and live the fantasy.

Ball M.C.: Op-u-lence!

See Also:

The Queen (1968), an earlier documentary about New York's drag pageants. An interesting look back at a time when it was even tougher to be out, gay, and in pumps.

PARTING GLANCES

(1986)

Written and directed by Bill Sherwood.
Richard Ganoung, John Bolger, Steve Buscemi, Kathy Kinney.
(First Run Features Home Video)

n the last 24 hours before Robert (Bolger) leaves behind his lover, Michael (Ganoung), for a two-year assignment in Africa, they have dinner with an older married couple and attend a going-away party for Robert thrown by their friend Joan (Kinney). Michael ducks out periodically to visit and prepare meals for his ex, Nick (Buscemi), who is battling AIDS. Truths are told as everyone tries to figure out what they're going to do next.

★ ★

One of the rules in gay journalism is to never call anything "the first gay something," because there always winds up being a previous gay something. So while *Parting Glances* isn't the first American gay movie, it was definitely a groundbreaker. For once, here was a gay movie that wasn't *about* gayness at all; it's just a story about two lovers and their friends and the people in their lives. Besides the sharp script, much of the fun in the movie lies in the early glimpses of Buscemi (before he became the king of indie cinema) and Kinney (years prior to her yukking it up on *Newhart* and *The Drew Carey Show*). The spot-on Ganoung deserved to have a much better career on the basis of his performance here. Writer-director Sherwood, tragically, died of complications from AIDS before getting to make another movie, but his legacy exists in the existence of American queer cinema itself, much of which couldn't have happened had the sweet and perceptive *Parting Glances* not gotten there first. (He passed the baton in a more literal way by hiring young Christine Vachon as an assistant editor; she went on to become a key figure as producer of all of Todd Haynes's films as well as *Swoon* (p. 204), *Camp* (p. 40), *Go Fish* (p. 95), *Boys Don't Cry* (1999), and a host of others.

Quotes to Remember:

> **Michael:** I have a secret.
> **Joan:** Hmm?
> **Michael:** I've always loved Nick more than Robert.
> **Joan:** I know.
> **Michael:** I've never told Nick.
> **Joan:** You better.

> **Nick:** You know the difference between straight guys and gay guys?
> **Michael:** I forget.
> **Nick:** There is none. This is a scary and seldom understood fact. Straight guys are jerks. Gay guys are jerks.

PEE-WEE'S BIG ADVENTURE

(1985)

Written by Phil Hartman, Paul Reubens, and Michael Varhol.
Directed by Tim Burton.
Paul Reubens, E.G. Daily, Mark Holton, Diane Salinger, Alice Nunn,
Jan Hooks, Jason Hervey. (Warner Bros. Home Entertainment)

Pee-wee (Reubens) sets off on a cross-country search after his supercool bike gets stolen by obnoxious rich kid Francis (Holton). Along the way, he encounters hitchhikers, ghostly truckers, an obnoxious Alamo tour guide, and a motorcycle gang. Finally, his exploits are turned into a movie in which James Brolin plays superspy "P.W.," whose experimental motorcycle must be recovered from enemy agents.

★ ★

One of the most brilliant comic creations ever, Pee-wee Herman is the ultimate man-child. An adult in an ill-fitting suit—and just a touch of makeup—Pee-wee lives for toys and novelties and childish observations, although he clearly gets a lot of fun out of life. He has girls who are friends—like Dottie (Daily) at the bike store—but he gets very uncomfortable when they start talking about kissing and love stuff. (Morgan Fairchild, as the Dottie in the movie-within-the-movie, gets much more action off of Brolin than Pee-wee would ever give the

Paul Reubens (Pee-wee Herman)

"real" Dottie.) This visual extravaganza put both Reubens and director Tim Burton on the map, and it remains among their best work.

Quotes to Remember:

> It's hard to capture the genius of this movie without hearing it in Pee-wee's voice, but I'll share this exchange:
>
> **Pee-wee:** I wouldn't sell my bike for all the money in the world. Not for a hundred million, billion, trillion dollars!
>
> **Francis:** Then you're crazy!
>
> **Pee-wee:** I know you are but what am I?

Francis: You're a nerd!

Pee-wee: I know you are but what am I?

Francis: You're an idiot!

Pee-wee: I know you are but what am I?

Both: I know you are but what am I? I know you are but what am I? I know you are but what am I?

Pee-wee: Infinity!

Francis: No, I'm not.

Both: You are! No way! Knock it off! Cut it out!

Francis: Shut up, Pee-wee!

Pee-wee: Why don't you make me?

Francis: You make me!

Pee-wee: Because. I don't make monkeys, I just train 'em.

Francis: Pee-wee, listen to reason.

[Pee-wee puts his hand to his ear]

Francis: Pee-wee!

Pee-wee: Shh! I'm listening to reason.

Francis: Pee-wee!

Pee-wee: That's my name, don't wear it out.

Francis: Remember the first time I saw your bike? You came riding past my house and I came running out to tell you how much I liked it even way back then?

Pee-wee: I love that story.

Fun facts:

★ Cassandra Peterson, best known as "Elvira, Mistress of the Dark," plays the female biker. She's an old friend of Reubens's from their days in Los Angeles's famed Groundlings comedy troupe.

★ If the head nun looks familiar, that's because she's played by Lynne Marie Stewart, who played Miss Yvonne on *Pee-wee's Playhouse* (and in the stage production on which it was based, *The Pee-wee Herman Show*).

See Also:

For a full dose of the magic that is Pee-wee, track down the
DVDs of the classic *Pee-wee's Playhouse* TV series. And make the
Pee-wee Christmas Special part of your holidays.

THE PILLOW BOOK

(1996)

Written by Peter Greenaway,
based on the book by Sei Shonagon.
Directed by Peter Greenaway.
Vivian Wu, Ewan McGregor, Yoshi Oida, Ken Ogata.
(Sony Pictures Home Entertainment)

Because her father would write on her face every year for her birthday, Nagiko (Wu) has a fetish for having her entire body written upon. The men she meets are either young enough to be good lovers but poor calligraphers or are old experts at writing who cannot fulfill her sexually. Then she meets Jerome (McGregor), a multilingual translator. It is he who encourages her to become "the pen as well as the paper," and she begins writing. Her work is initially turned down by the publisher (Oida) who forced her writer father (Ogata) into sexual servitude, but he responds favorably when she submits her text written on a naked Jerome. Jerome loses both Nagiko and the publisher as his two lovers begin a cat-and-mouse game with her texts. Ultimately, Nagiko will have her revenge on the man who destroyed both her father and her lover.

★ ★

Vivian Wu (Nagiko) and Ewan McGregor (Jerome)

A word about the penis: It seems to be all but invisible in the mainstream cinema. Entire feminist texts have probably been written about whether this is because the patriarchy doesn't want to face its own latent homosexuality or whether internal genitals are more pleasing to artists than the external kind. In any event, director Peter Greenaway has no hang-ups about the male genitalia, particularly in *The Pillow Book*. And while Ewan McGregor's manly bits may be worth the price of admission—you can also see them in *Trainspotting* (1996) and *Velvet Goldmine* (1998)—they're hardly the only reason to see this fascinating art film. Like Greta Scacchi's artist character in *The Player* (1992), Greenaway sees the visual artistic possibilities of text (be it letters, characters, numbers even) and marries it to the beauty of the human body. Greenaway has long posited that the cinema is too rich a medium "to be left to the storytellers," and he creates complex, gorgeous art on celluloid. See it on the big screen if you can, but even on video, *The Pillow Book* is a visual feast.

PRICK UP YOUR EARS

(1987)

Written by Alan Bennett,
based on the book by John Lahr.
Directed by Stephen Frears.
Gary Oldman, Alfred Molina, Vanessa Redgrave, Frances Barber,
Wallace Shawn, Julie Walters. (MGM Home Entertainment)

American author John Lahr (Shawn) comes to England to write a biography about notorious British playwright Joe Orton (Oldman), who was the popular bad boy of the London stage in the 1960s until he was murdered by his lover Kenneth Halliwell (Molina). Orton's agent, Peggy Ramsay (Redgrave), gives Lahr access to Orton's diaries, where we discover that Orton began as a young would-be actor, taken under Ken's wing. While Joe flourished as both a writer and a cocksman—he was a regular practitioner of "cottaging," or finding sex in public restrooms—Ken grew more bitter and diminished until he finally killed Joe and himself.

★ ★

A blatantly open pre-Stonewall gay man, Joe Orton shook up British conventions both on and off the stage. This loving biopic captures a man who is both a creative (and naughty) wit and an unapologetically sexual bloke. The cruising sequences here—later parodied on TV's *Strangers with Candy*—are better than anything in *Cruising* (see p. 58) at capturing the electricity and thrill of the hunt for (and acquisition of) anonymous sex. *Prick* also succeeds at the more difficult task of showing why Joe remained in the same little flat with Ken even after reaching success on his own. Alan Bennett's script goes leaps and bounds above the standard dreary biopic, and Oldman and Molina give us an insight into these two men who resented each other but couldn't seem to live without each other either.

Quotes to Remember:

Policeman (upon discovering the bodies of Joe and Ken): Dear, oh, dear. Somebody here has been playing silly buggers.

Peggy (to John, about the '60s): It was the Dark Ages. Men and men. And they could still put you in prison for it. And they did, dear.

Joe (repelling Ken's advances): No. Have a wank.
Ken: Have a wank? I can't just have a wank! I need three days' notice to have a wank! You can just stand there and do it. Me, it's like organizing D Day. Forces have to be assembled, magazines bought, the past dredged for some unsuitably unsavory episode, the dogged thought of which can still produce a faint flicker of desire. Have a wank—it'd be easier to raise the Titanic. And don't write it down!

Anthea Lahr (reading teenage Orton's diary): "Woke up late. Did not go to school. Told Mum I felt sick. When she'd gone to work, I listened to *Housewives' Choice*."
Anthea's mum [translating the passages written in shorthand]:

"Then went into Mum's bedroom and arranged the dressing table mirrors and had a lovely, long, slow wink."

Anthea: "Wink." Are you sure that's an "i"?

Anthea's mum: No, dear, I'm not sure at all.

Ken (to Joe): I don't understand my life. I was an only child. I lost both my parents. By the time I was 20 I was going bald. I'm a homosexual. In the way of circumstances and background, I had everything an artist could possibly want. It was practically a blueprint. I was programmed to be a novelist or a playwright. But I'm not, and you are!

Peggy: Ken was the first wife. Did all the work and the waiting, and then... [sighs]

John: Well, first wives don't usually beat their husbands' heads in.

Peggy: No. Though why, I can't think.

John: So what does that make you? The second wife?

Peggy: Better than that, dear. The widow.

See Also:

Frears's *My Beautiful Laundrette* (1985), an unlikely love story between an ambitious Pakistani immigrant (Gordon Warnecke) and a street punk (Daniel Day-Lewis) looking for honest work. While much of Hanif Kureishi's script clangs in its anti-Thatcherite speechifying, the film remains sexy and clever.

ROCK HUDSON'S HOME MOVIES

(1992)

Written and directed by Mark Rappaport.
Eric Farr. (Water Bearer Films Home Video)

Rock Hudson (Farr) appears from beyond the grave to show the clips from his lengthy film career that prove that his homosexuality, an open secret in Hollywood's golden age, was up there on the screen all along. And taken out of context, these clips do indeed advertise Hudson's sexuality in the midst of otherwise innocuous films. Rappaport explores everything from the eternal Rock-Doris Day-Tony Randall triangle to Rock's seemingly endless series of interrupted kisses with his female costars. Funny, sad, and provocative, *Rock Hudson's Home Movies* provides an alternative look at one of the movies' great gay icons.

★ ★

In *Home Movies* and the later, more polished, compilations *From the Journals of Jean Seberg* (1995) and *The Silver Screen: Color Me Lavender* (1997), out filmmaker Rappaport creates extraordinary collages that mix movie images, both in and out of context, with the real lives of the people up there on the screen. While the notion that Hudson's gayness was a part of his movies might seem obvious in movies like *Pillow Talk* (1959), in which he pretends to be gay to seduce Doris Day, or *Man's Favorite Sport?* (1964), where he plays a fishing expert who can't stand to fish and doesn't like the, uh, smell of fish, *Home Movies* digs deeper, recontextualizing moments where Hudson cruises his costars (including John Wayne!) and even predicts his eventual death from AIDS-related complications. The film will make you rethink the way you look at Rock Hudson—and at movies in general—while exploring the codes and veils of secrecy that shrouded gay men for most of the 20th century.

Quotes to Remember:

"Rock": In a sense, Tony is as much my significant other as Doris is.

"Rock": It's not like it wasn't up there on the screen—if you watched the films carefully.

See Also:

You'll want to run out and view (or closely review) lots of Hudson's movies after seeing this one, but let me point out the hoary 1965 comedy *A Very Special Favor*, in which Rock pretends to be a big nellie poof to seduce icy shrink Leslie Caron. (It's the one obvious movie that Rappaport somehow missed.) And I can't recommend Rappaport's *From the Journals of Jean Seberg* highly enough for anyone who loves films, particularly for its reflections on how screen images and backstage gossip exist intertwined in our movie memories.

SAVED!

(2004)

Written by Brian Dannelly and Michael Urban.
Directed by Brian Dannelly.
Jena Malone, Mandy Moore, Patrick Fugit, Eva Amurri,
Macaulay Culkin, Heather Mattarazzo, Martin Donovan,
Mary-Louise Parker. (MGM Home Entertainment)

Mary (Malone) is one of her Christian high school's popular girls, but her life changes when she gets pregnant during senior year. It's not entirely her fault, of course: Her boyfriend Dean (Chad Faust) admitted that he thought he might be gay, and after bumping her head she had a vision of Jesus telling her to do everything she could to save him. Soon after they have sex, though, he gets dragged off to Mercy House for "de-gayification." Mary winds up becoming close friends with outcasts Cassandra (Amurri) and Roland (Culkin) while battling former best friend Hillary Faye (Moore) for the affections of hunky Christian skateboarder Patrick (Fugit).

★ ★

While the satire could have been more biting in this comedy about Christian fundamentalism, *Saved!* offers a talented ensemble cast and a wicked look at consumer-culture religion, complete with Bible-quoting boy bands and skateboarding missionaries. The gay characters are fairly peripheral and exist more to serve the plot—despite the fact that cowriter-director Dannelly is queer—but this tart teen comedy explores the closing of the American mind and the insidiousness of religion's easy answers. The droll Amurri makes a great pair with Culkin, out actress Matarazzo is brilliantly creepy as the social-climbing Tia, and Donovan is hilarious as a with-it adult whose attempts at teen slang are just the tiniest bit tin-eared. While Malone gives the film an appealing center, it's Moore as the ultimate holier-than-thou diva who steals the show. (Furious at Mary, Hillary Faye heaves a Bible at her back while shouting, "I am *filled* with Christ's love!") For the great many gay men who have had to overcome the bigotry of fundamentalism in their past, *Saved!* will remind them of what they have managed to save themselves from.

Quotes to Remember:

Tia: Hey, Mary. Sorry to hear about Dean's faggotry.

Hillary Faye: Nobody's born a gay. They're born *again*, right?

Hillary Faye: I've been doing "the Christian thing" all my life. I did not have sex with a gay and try and blame it on Jesus!

SCARY MOVIE

(2000)

**Written by Shawn Wayans and Marlon Wayans & Buddy Johnson
and Phil Beuman & Jason Friedberg and Aaron Seltzer.
Directed by Keenen Ivory Wayans.**
Anna Faris, Shawn Wayans,
Marlon Wayans, Shannon Elizabeth, Cheri Oteri.
(Miramax Home Entertainment)

This very silly spoof of *Scream* (1996) and *I Know What You Did Last Summer* (1997) trots out the *Airplane!* (1980) style of scattershot parody, to varying degrees of success. What makes it interesting is Shawn Wayans's Ray character, a high school football stud who's very obviously gay, although he never acknowledges it, and the people around him never quite figure it out either. It's that obliviousness that's played for laughs here, and not the homosexuality itself, which represents a big leap for any movie with the name "Wayans" on it. I still cringe at the thought of the Damon Wayans–scripted *Mo' Money* (1992), which featured a blisteringly offensive scene in which Damon and Marlon Wayans play a pair of simpering queens talking about AIDS; mainstream African-American comedies of the '80s and '90s in general, and Wayans family movies in particular, could generally be counted upon to be homophobic at least in passing. It would be nice to see that change.

See Also:

Robert Townsend's *Hollywood Shuffle* (1987), cowritten by Keenen Ivory Wayans. How's this for some irony: The whole movie is about how Hollywood has demeaned blacks for decades by giving African-American actors and actresses nothing to play but embarrassing stereotypes, and the movie's one gay character is a bitchy, prissy, man-hungry hairdresser who is the butt of the hero's scorn. In other words—a stereotype.

SCORE

(1973)

Written by Jerry Douglas,
based on his play.
Directed by Radley Metzger.
Claire Wilbur, Calvin Culver, Lynn Lowry, Gerald Grant, Carl Parker.
(First Run Features Home Video)

S winging couple Elvira (Wilbur) and Jack (Grant) have a bet to see whether or not she can seduce innocent young Betsy (Lowry), who is somewhat frustrated in her marriage to strapping, sexually confused Eddie (Culver). Elvira seduces telephone repairman Mike (Parker) in front of Betsy, who is both shocked and intrigued. Eddie and Betsy come over to Elvira and Jack's for dinner, and the foursome get stoned and try on fantasy costumes. Elvira and Betsy go upstairs while Jack and Eddie go downstairs. Who will score?

★ ★

Viva la sexual revolution! While *Score* is occasionally just a little too archly winky-winky for its own good, this little fable about sexual fidelity and fluidity remains a lot sexier and a lot less dated than you'd think three decades later. It seems almost unthinkable in this day and age to make a soft-core sex flick—although a more hard-core version of this movie, featuring some edited gay scenes, may yet surface—that prominently features two men winding up in bed together. You can't tune into late-night Cinemax or a hotel Spectravision channel without getting some glammed-up girl-on-girl action, but two guys together remains taboo. Perhaps not surprisingly, two of *Score*'s players went on to greater fame in the world of gay porn—Calvin Culver became a huge star under the name Casey Donovan while writer Douglas continues to be one of queer smut's most creative and ambitious writer-directors.

Fun fact:

★ The original stage production of *Score* featured none other than a young Sylvester Stallone in the role of the telephone repairman.

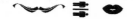

SHOW ME LOVE
(FUCKING ÅMÅL)

(1998)

Written and directed by Lukas Moodysson.
Alexandra Dahlström, Rebecka Liljeberg, Erica Carlson, Mathias Rust.
(Strand Releasing Home Video)

A gnes (Liljeberg) is introverted, friendless, and—it's whispered in the halls of her high school—a lesbian. She pines for the attractive and restless Elin (Dahlström), who's dying to get out of their boring town of Åmål. Elin winds up being one of the few guests to show up for Agnes's birthday party; she kisses Agnes on a bet but immediately runs away. Feeling guilty about it, Elin returns that night (as Agnes is trying to slash her wrists with a disposable razor) and the two eventually kiss for real. Afraid of social ostracism, Elin ignores Agnes and starts going out with nice-guy Johan (Rust), but she can't deny her attraction to the uncool girl who has captured her fancy. Ultimately, in front of the entire school, they come out...of the ladies' room. (Trust me, you have to see it for yourself.)

★★★★★★★★★★★★★★★★★★★★★★★★★★★★★★

This charming Swedish romantic comedy is an understated delight. Like a Scandinavian Alexander Payne, the very talented Moodysson has a masterful eye for both the beauty and drab-

Rebecka Liljeberg (Agnes) and Alexandra Dahlström (Elin)

ness of everyday life. His characters exist in a world that feels very much like our own, and subsequently their problems and triumphs feel like they're ours as well. The awkwardness of teenage life—where absolutely everything in one's life can change over the course of just one week—is nailed just perfectly. The sweet ending will put you in a swoony mood.

See Also:

Moodysson's next film, the joyous *Together* (2000), captures life in a Swedish commune circa 1975 and also includes interesting gay and lesbian characters. *Late Bloomers*, from Julia and Gretchen Dyer, is another great lesbian coming-out movie, only this time the protagonists are two middle-aged schoolworkers in the Dallas suburbs. And while it's not as good as *Show Me Love*, the 1995 comedy *The Incredibly True Adventure of Two Girls in Love* is also a nice little coming-of-age tale.

SHOWGIRLS

(1995)

Written by Joe Eszterhas.
Directed by Paul Verhoeven.
Elizabeth Berkley, Gina Gershon, Kyle MacLachlan, Robert Davi,
Gina Ravera, Glenn Plummer, Lin Tucci, Alan Rachins, Patrick Bristow.
(MGM Home Entertainment)

Ex-prostitute Nomi Malone (Berkley) comes to Las Vegas to become a dancer. She winds up working in a sleazy strip joint, the Cheetah, but she dreams of joining the cast of *Goddess*, a splashy extravaganza being staged in the Stardust hotel, on the strip. Nomi joins the chorus of *Goddess* and climbs the showbiz ladder, locking horns along the way with diva leading lady Cristal (Gershon). Dancer James (Plummer) tells Nomi she is wasting her talent. After knocking Cristal out of the way—literally—to become the star of *Goddess*, Nomi realizes it's rotten at the top and flees town. Next stop? Hollywood.

★ ★

People throw around the word "worst" with some abandon when discussing movies, so let me quote the TV producer from Gillian Armstrong's delightful cult musical *Starstruck* (1982), who observes, "There's only boring and interesting." And no matter what your feelings about the very infamous *Showgirls*, it sure as shit ain't boring. I can't quite go with critic Charles Taylor and legendary French director Jacques Rivette, who praise *Showgirls* as a work of art, saying that Eszterhas and Verhoeven set out to make a film this crass and vulgar because crassness and vulgarity are what Vegas is all about.

On the other hand, I think too many gay men are far too dismissive of this movie; in hooting it off the screen as though it were the second coming of *Valley of the Dolls* (see p. 216), they miss the elements that do, indeed, work. For one thing, there's Gershon's delicious and knowingly scenery-chewing performance as the ravenously bisexual Cristal. As many critics have pointed out, Gershon is the one person who knows what movie she's in, and she gives Eszterhas's loony dialogue the handling it deserves. And while the jury may be out on Berkley, you have to give her credit for completely committing to the role. From her naked cavorting to her stripper-pole licking, she's in it to win it. (And her career is still trying to survive it.) If there's one element that keeps *Showgirls* from being a total hoot—for me, anyway—it's the brutal third-act rape scene of Molly (Ravera), the film's one genuinely nice character. This violent violation would fit in naturally in just about any of Verhoeven's other gritty and intense movies, but it sticks out unpleasantly in *Showgirls'* otherwise cartoonish atmosphere. In any event, whether you're laughing at it or taking it at face value, *Showgirls* is a glorious crime whose scene you'll return to again and again.

Quotes to Remember:

Sleazy guy in casino (to Nomi): You lose all your money, honey? You wanna make some more? It won't take you any longer than 15 minutes. [She stalks off.] Sooner or later you're gonna have to sell it!

James (about Nomi's lap dancing): Man, everybody got AIDS and shit. What is it that you think you do? You fuck 'em without fucking 'em. That's what you do. Well it ain't right! You've got too much talent for it to be right!

Tony [dance director of *Goddess*]: I don't care whether you live or die. I want to see you dance. I want to see you smile. I can't use you if you can't smile; I can't use you if you can't show; I can't use you if you can't sell.

James (about Nomi leaving the Cheetah to do *Goddess*): You don't want to be in this kind of show. What you're doing, at least it's honest. They want tits and ass; you give them tits and ass. Here, they pretend they want something else, and you *still* show them tits and ass.

Cristal: You have great tits. They're really beautiful.
Nomi: Thank you.
Cristal: I like nice tits. Always have. How 'bout you?
Nomi: I like having nice tits.
Cristal: How do you like having 'em?
Nomi: What do you mean?
Cristal: You know what I mean.
Nomi: I like having them in a nice dress or a tight top.
Cristal: You like to show 'em off.
Nomi: I didn't like showing them off at the Cheetah.
Cristal: Why not? I liked looking at 'em there. Everybody liked looking at 'em there.
Nomi: Made me feel like a hooker.
Cristal: You are a whore, darlin'.
Nomi: No I'm not.
Cristal: We all are. We take the cash, we cash the check, we show them what they want to see.
Nomi: Maybe you are a whore, Cristal, but I'm not.
Cristal: You and me? We're exactly alike.

Henrietta: She looks better than a 10-inch dick, and you know it!

Al [Nomi's former boss at the Cheetah, after seeing her in *Goddess*]: Must be weird not having anybody come on you.

SKIDOO

(1968)

Written by Doran William Cannon.
Directed by Otto Preminger.
Jackie Gleason, Carol Channing, Frankie Avalon,
Groucho Marx, John Philip Law, Cesar Romero, Michael Constantine,
Alexandra Hay, Mickey Rooney, Austin Pendleton.
(Not available on home video—write Paramount and complain)

Former gangster Tony (Gleason) is called upon by mob boss "God" (Marx) to go into prison and bump off moneyman "Blue Chips" Packard (Rooney), who is about to turn state's evidence. Tony's wife, Flo (Channing), investigates his disappearance by grilling up-and-coming goodfella Angie (Avalon). With the help of his cellmate, Fred (Pendleton), Tony escapes prison by slipping LSD into everyone's food and making a hot-air balloon out of garbage cans and frozen-food bags. Flo—aided by daughter Darlene (Hay) and her boyfriend, Stash (Law)—leads a flotilla of hippies to God's yacht to rescue Tony.

★ ★

You know how embarrassing it is when your parents try to use young hipster slang? The cinematic equivalent would have to be this freaky-deaky would-be comedy, which tries to marry Hollywood's old guard with what the codgers thought was, like, groovy hippie stuff. *Skidoo* makes a fascinating cultural artifact in that the establishment rarely gets it this wrong when they're trying to co-opt the counterculture. As faggotry gets diluted by the *Birdcage*s (1996) and the *In & Out*s (1997) of the world, it's good to hone your eyes for movies that have no feel whatsoever for the subcultures they're exploiting. Besides, any movie that features Jackie Gleason taking an acid trip, Carol Channing stripping out of a zip-around Rudi Gernreich dress to seduce Frankie Avalon, and Nilsson singing the entire closing credits (down to the "Copyright M-C-M-L-X-V-I-I-I") is worth seeking out.

SMILE

(1975)

Written by Jerry Belson.
Directed by Michael Ritchie.
Bruce Dern, Barbara Feldon, Annette O'Toole, Nicholas Pryor,
Michael Kidd, Colleen Camp, Melanie Griffith,
Maria O'Brien. (MGM Home Entertainment)

California's annual Young American Miss pageant comes to Santa Rosa. It's a very big deal for former YAM Brenda DiCarlo (Feldon), who's running the preparations despite getting very little help from her ever-surlier and ever-drunker husband Andy (Pryor). But who can blame Andy for being sick of the pageant? When he's not being hectored by Brenda at home, he has to deal with his best friend Big Bob (Dern), the head judge and a constant spouter of feel-good clichés. The girls are a mixed bag of the talented, the cynical, and the clueless. And this year they hired a "Hollywood professional," Tommy French (Kidd), to choreograph. Cue the wholesomeness!

★ ★

One of the most abused words of this generation—besides *camp* and *surreal*—is *satire*. The term gets applied to anything that's a spoof, basically, but real, hard-hitting, hilarious satire is hard to come by. Michael Ritchie's *Smile* subtly but devastatingly lacerates America's ability to lie to itself and to others under a veneer of fake charm, can-do boosterism, and, of course, smiles. If you sometimes wonder what prompted the last few decades of

American irony, *Smile* will remind you. There's no downturn in life so serious that it can't be addressed with a T-shirt-ready aphorism, and no function of human sexuality that can't be reduced to a sniggering cocktail novelty. From its landscape of Denny's and VA auditoriums to its stultifying Jaycees luncheons, *Smile*'s Santa Rosa is America. And the girls are all trying to succeed in it by any means necessary. Even if you're not one of those dudes who are glued to the set every year for the Miss America pageant, you'll appreciate the blistering brilliance of this razor-sharp film.

SOME LIKE IT HOT

(1959)

Written by Billy Wilder and I.A.L. Diamond.
Directed by Billy Wilder.
Jack Lemmon, Tony Curtis, Marilyn Monroe, Joe E. Brown,
George Raft, Pat O'Brien, Joan Shawlee.
(MGM Home Entertainment)

After accidentally witnessing the St. Valentine's Day Massacre, musicians Joe (Curtis) and Jerry (Lemmon) flee Chicago mobsters by joining an all-girl band, Sweet Sue and Her Society Synchopators, and heading to Florida disguised as "Josephine" and "Daphne." They both fall for band singer Sugar Kane (Monroe). Joe woos Sugar by pretending to be rich while "Daphne" attracts the attention of actual millionaire Osgood Fielding (Brown). The Illinois gangsters wind up in Florida, leading to chases, more disguises, and even more revelations.

★ ★

From Sugar's lament that she always winds up with "the fuzzy end of the lollipop" to Osgood's nonplussed reaction to "Daphne's" true gender—the immortal closing line, "Well—

nobody's perfect"—*Some Like It Hot* is a dizzying farce whose sexual content remains provocative and funny a half century later. While the film's whole hiding-out-in-drag concept has been stolen a thousand times over, no one else has taken the story to the heights that Wilder and Diamond accomplished. For one thing, camouflage dominates the story even before Joe and Jerry put on dresses—a funeral home is actually a speakeasy, for instance, where high-proof "coffee" is served. By the time the story gets to Florida, we have fake-millionaire Joe using Osgood's yacht (and Cary Grant's voice) to seduce Sugar, who pretends to be a Bryn Mawr girl. And Jack Lemmon's "Daphne," during all this, comes to enjoy his masquerade, reveling in the attention and gifts lavished upon him. (The fact that he chooses the alias "Daphne," rather than "Geraldine," reveals the character's willingness to gender-bend.) Boasting wonderfully clever banter and a dollop of movie inside jokes, *Hot* is still one of the great American film comedies.

Quotes to Remember:

> **Sue:** There are two things that I will not put up with during working hours. One is liquor, and the other is men!
> **"Daphne":** Men?
> **"Josephine":** Oh, you don't have to worry about that.
> **"Daphne":** We wouldn't be caught dead with men! Rough, hairy beasts...with eight hands! And they all just want one thing from a girl.

> [Joe returns from his date with Sugar to find Jerry-"Daphne" having returned from a date with Osgood]
> **Jerry:** Have I got things to tell you...
> **Joe:** What happened?
> **Jerry:** I'm engaged.
> **Joe:** Congratulations. Who's the lucky girl?

Jerry: I am.

Joe: What?

Jerry: Osgood proposed to me. We're planning a June wedding.

Joe: What are you talking about? You can't marry Osgood.

Jerry: You think he's too old for me?

Joe: Jerry, you can't be serious!

Jerry: Why not? He keeps marrying girls all the time!

Joe: But you're not a girl, you're a guy! And why would a guy want to marry a guy?

Jerry: Security!

SOUTH PARK: BIGGER, LONGER & UNCUT

(1999)

Written by Trey Parker and Matt Stone and Pam Brady;
songs by Trey Parker and Marc Shaiman.
Directed by Trey Parker.
Trey Parker, Matt Stone, Mary Kay Bergman,
Isaac Hayes, George Clooney. (Paramount Home Video)

I n this R-rated adaptation of the popular TV show, the children of South Park flock to see the R-rated adaptation of the popular Canadian TV show *Terrance & Philip*. The movie's rampant profanity turns all the kids into potty-mouths, much to the concern of their parents and teachers. Led by Kyle's mom, Sheila, the parents declare war on Canada and plan to execute Terrance & Philip, not realizing that doing so will open the seventh seal and allow Satan and his gay lover, Saddam Hussein, to rule the earth for two million years of darkness.

★ ★

It's profane, it's apocalyptic, and it's a musical. This big-screen adaptation of the crudely-animated TV hit brilliantly satirizes uptight moralists who use children as their excuse for censorship while also mocking the conventions of the musical. (And in doing so, *South Park* wound up being one of the best movie musicals of the late 20th century.) Sure, Satan's gay, but he winds up being one of the film's more likable characters, what with his giant Skeet Ulrich poster and the fact that Saddam is so mean to him. Satan even gets the movie's big "I wish" number, "Up There." South Park kids Kyle, Stan, and Cartman, meanwhile, try to save the day—because they know that's what their hero, flamboyant figure skater Brian Boitano, would do. Naughty, offensive, and smart, *South Park: Bigger, Longer & Uncut* proves that neither musicals nor animated features have to be dull, safe, or even family-friendly.

Quotes to Remember:

> **Mr. Garrison:** How would you like to go see the school counselor?
> **Cartman:** How would you like to suck my balls?
> **Mr. Garrison** (shocked): What did you say?
> **Cartman:** I'm sorry, I'm sorry. Actually, what I said was [pulls out bullhorn], HOW WOULD YOU LIKE TO SUCK MY BALLS?

> **Satan** (crying): It's Saddam. He doesn't nurture my emotions. He just wants sex, and he can't learn to communicate.

> **Sheila:** Men, when you're out there on the battlefield and you're looking into the beady eyes of a Canadian, as he charges you with his hockey stick or whatever he has, and people are dying all around you, just remember what the [Motion Picture Association of America] says—horrific, deplorable violence is OK as long as people don't say naughty words. That is what this war is all about!

All: Thank God we live in this quiet, little, pissant, redneck, Podunk, jerkwater, greenhorn, one-horse, mudhole, peckerwood, right-wing, whistle-stop, hobnail, truck-driving, old-fashioned, hayseed, inbred, unkempt, out-of-date, out-of-touch, white-trash, kick-ass mountain town!

A
STAR
IS
BORN

(1954)

Written by Moss Hart,
based on the screenplay by Dorothy Parker,
Alan Campbell, and William A. Wellman,
from the story by William A. Wellman and Robert Carson.
Directed by George Cukor.
Judy Garland, James Mason, Jack Carson,
Charles Bickford, Tommy Noonan. (Warner Home Video)

Singer Esther Blodgett (Garland) is discovered by alcoholic movie star Norman Maine (Mason), who gets her a screen test at his studio. Renamed Vicki Lester by the studio bosses, she becomes a big musical star. Maine, meanwhile, is let go because his drinking makes him too much of a liability. Esther stands by Norman, but when he realizes that his demons might destroy her career as well, he commits suicide. Esther is despondent, but her friend Danny (Noonan) reminds her that Norman sacrificed everything for her, his greatest creation, and she owes it to his memory to go on in his honor. She appears at a charity event, the one where she and Norman first met years earlier, and introduces herself to the audience as "Mrs. Norman Maine."

★★★★★★★★★★★★★★★★★★★★★★★★★★★★★★★

Making fun of old queens for loving Judy Garland is like making fun of the French for liking Jerry Lewis—it's a cliché, and it's insulting to a talented performer. In Garland's case, she's definitely one of the 20th century's greatest singers. It may be old-hat for gays to love her for her suffering, but there's no reason why we can't still appreciate her enormous talents as a singer and as an actress. By teaming up with gay director George Cukor to make *A Star Is Born*, Garland had what's probably her greatest film role. She runs an amazing emotional gamut while also singing a series of unforgettable Harold Arlen-Ira Gershwin songs. In *The Advocate*, Dave White wrote about her searing performance of "The Man That Got Away": "I not only heard her sing but saw her entire body heave forward off the screen while she did it. The woman lunged at her audience like she was having a fit, like a female Johnny Rotten. It reminded me of seeing my favorite band, Sonic Youth, the first time back in the '80s, and being turned inside out by their noise, being made to feel as if my head would explode. Judy Garland had just done the same thing to me. And she was dead, a recording; she was doing it from a piece of 50-year-old film." And *that's* why Judy Garland still matters, despite the best efforts of some contemporary fags to turn her into a pop-culture punch line.

See Also:

All three versions of *A Star Is Born* merit a look: The original 1937 version boasts great performances from Janet Gaynor and Fredric March—plus a screenplay cowritten by Dorothy Parker—and the 1976 Barbra Streisand disaster is rife with unintentional humor. And if you're really in the mood to dig into the series, all three movies are loosely based on Cukor's 1932 *What Price Hollywood?*

SUDDENLY, LAST SUMMER

(1959)

Written by Gore Vidal,
based on the play by Tennessee Williams.
Directed by Joseph L. Mankiewicz.
Katharine Hepburn, Montgomery Clift, Elizabeth Taylor.
(Sony Pictures Home Entertainment)

n 1937 wealthy widow Violet Venable (Hepburn), who clings
desperately to the memory of her late son Sebastian, offers
to make a sizable contribution toward the work of Dr.
Cukrowicz (Clift) if he will perform a lobotomy on her niece,
Catherine (Taylor), whom Violet claims has been "babbling
obscenities" ever since Sebastian's death. Catherine was with
Sebastian when he died during a trip to Europe, but the event
was so traumatizing that she cannot bring herself to remember
it. Cukrowicz discovers that Sebastian used Violet and then—
after his mother became too old—Catherine as bait to attract
men during these trips. And finally, Catherine brings herself to
recall the horrifying circumstances of Sebastian's death.

★ ★

Ah, the delicious overripeness of Tennessee Williams. His
Southern gothic tales of madness often include homosexuality,
bizarre sexual violence, and lurid creepiness, and that's part of

why we love him so. Those plot elements, however, made it awfully difficult to bring his hit plays to the screen in the 1950s, so it's interesting to watch writers go through hoops to say things without saying things. Even in the hands of a talent like Vidal, it's exquisitely bizarre to watch these characters talk about rape, incest, cannibalism, and such without addressing them head-on. But hey, it's got Liz Taylor in a white bathing suit, Montgomery Clift sporting his disturbing post-car-accident face, Hepburn wrapping her voice around the purplest of prose, and a faggot so evil the movie never even dares show us his face.

See Also:

Vidal's reminiscences about this film is just one of many reasons to see *The Celluloid Closet* (see p. 50). Mankiewicz, in addition to the legendary *All About Eve* (see p. 1), made scads of other entertaining films, including *Sleuth, A Letter to Three Wives* (1949), and the legendary Taylor-Burton money-loser *Cleopatra* (1963).

SUNDAY BLOODY SUNDAY

(1971)

Written by Penelope Gilliatt.
Directed by John Schlesinger.
Peter Finch, Glenda Jackson, Murray Head, Peggy Ashcroft.
(MGM Home Entertainment)

Jewish doctor Daniel (Finch) loves artist Bob (Head). And so does divorcee Alex (Jackson). Daniel and Alex both know of their shared claim on Bob, but since Bob tends to run away from difficult discussions, they both know better than to talk about it with him. Eventually, both realize that Bob is incapable of commitment or a mature relationship, and they resign themselves to the fact that he is dashing off to New York for what promises to be an open-ended stay. Alex determines that she will soldier on without Bob; Daniel misses him.

★ ★

Because this is a movie about people not communicating, the silences and the delicate turns of phrase tell the real story here. Schlesinger deals with mature themes in a very frank matter for the period—the kiss between Finch and Head early on shocked 1971 audiences, no doubt because the director handles the moment in a very matter-of-fact way rather than signal to the audience that they're witnessing something taboo or groundbreaking. Jackson and Finch deliver some of the best work of their distinguished careers. I know Jackson has found fulfillment as a member of the British government, but I do so miss her onscreen; she has the best verbal sneer this side of Bette Davis, but she can turn on a dime to a vulnerable side that is shattering.

Fun Facts:

★ Murray Head went on to find fame in the stage musicals *Jesus Christ Superstar* and *Chess*; the latter brought him one-hit wonder fame with the song "One Night in Bangkok."

★ Screenwriter Penelope Gilliatt was also a film critic—she was best known in the United States as the fill-in for Pauline Kael at *The New Yorker* during the period that Kael went to Hollywood to work for Warren Beatty's production company.

★ Richard Loncraine, who plays one of Bob's artistic collaborators, went on to direct such films as *Brimstone & Treacle* (1982), *Wimbledon* (2004), and the extraordinary Ian McKellen version of *Richard III* (1995).

★ Given the triangle at the center of the film's story, the recurring musical theme is appropriately a trio from Mozart's *Cosi fan Tutte*.

Quotes to Remember:

Bob: We're free to do what we want.
Alex: Darling...other people often do what they don't want to do at all.

Alex: I've had this business—"anything is better than

nothing." There are times when nothing *has* to be better than anything.

See Also:

Openly gay director John Schlesinger's career includes several other classics, including *Darling* (1965), *Marathon Man* (1976), *and Cold Comfort Farm* (1995). (And yes, he won the Oscar for *Midnight Cowboy* (1969), but I've always found that movie overdone and subtly homophobic. But I'm clearly in the minority on that one.)

SUNRISE

(1927)

Written by Carl Mayer,
based on the novella "A Trip to Tilsit"
by Hermann Sudermann;
titles by Katherine Hilliker and H.H. Caldwell.
Directed by F.W. Murnau.
George O'Brien, Janet Gaynor, Margaret Livingston.
(Twentieth Century Fox Home Entertainment)

A farmer (O'Brien) neglects his wife (Gaynor) for the attentions of a woman from the city (Livingston). The woman suggests that he take his wife out in a boat and drown her. He tells his wife that they will take a trip to the city across the river, but when he tries to throw her overboard, he just can't do it. They make it to the other side, and the wife runs away from him. The two take a trolley into town and come upon a young couple getting married. Hearing the wedding vows again, the man is overcome with shame and repledges his love to his wife. After the two spend a magical day in the city, they take their boat back across the river. There is a storm, and the wife is thrown overboard. The husband leads a search party to no avail. The woman assumes he has carried out their plan, but when she goes to him, he attacks her in a rage. Before he can strangle the woman, news arrives that his wife has been saved. The woman returns to the city.

★ ★

"Oh, Mary, it takes a fairy to make something pretty," gushes Emory in *The Boys in the Band* (see p. 32), and that's certainly borne out by *Sunrise*, one of the most beautiful films ever made. Gay director F.W. Murnau was a giant of the silent cinema, and his movies still rank among the most memorable, daring, unforgettable ones ever made. While the subtitle of *Sunrise—A Song of Two Humans*—is the kind of thing no contemporary filmmaker could ever get away with, it's a perfect description for this lovely little tale. While it's not heavy on plot, *Sunrise* examines a couple that has grown estranged and how both people rediscover what made them fall in love in the first place. And visually, it's constantly stunning—watch how the in-love-again couple saunters through traffic without noticing the cars as the landscape around them (in their minds, anyway) becomes a country meadow. *Sunrise* opened the same year as *The Jazz Singer*, and film historians still wonder how much more visually sophisticated silent films might have become if movies hadn't suddenly been forced to get locked down around a microphone.

AUTEUR ALERT:

Before meeting his demise in a *Hollywood Babylon*-esque death that purportedly involved sex in a moving car with his houseboy, director Murnau made several unforgettable films, including *Nosferatu* (1922) and *The Last Laugh* (1924). If you've never had a college professor or film nerd friend sit you down to watch silent movies, these three Murnau classics are a great place to start.

SUNSET BLVD.

(1950)

**Written by Charles Brackett, Billy Wilder, and D.M. Marshman Jr.
Directed by Billy Wilder.**
Gloria Swanson, William Holden, Erich von Stroheim, Nancy Olson,
Cecil B. DeMille, Hedda Hopper. (Paramount Home Entertainment)

While ditching two repo men, down-on-his-luck screenwriter Joe Gillis (Holden) steers his car into a moldering Hollywood mansion owned by forgotten silent screen star Norma Desmond (Swanson). Norma has planned to make her comeback with *Salome*, and she hires Joe to stay on and help her write the screenplay. Before long, he is being kept by her, even though he starts sneaking out at night to work on his own screenplay with Betty (Olson), who falls in love with him. Joe finds out that Norma's butler Max (Von Stroheim) was once her director and her husband, and that it is Max who writes the fan letters Norma thinks her public is still sending her. When Joe tries to leave, Norma shoots him; as the newsreel cameras arrive at the scene of the crime, she snaps and becomes convinced that shooting on *Salome* has finally begun.

★ ★

While the name Norma Desmond and the line "I'm ready for my closeup, Mr. DeMille" have become part of the vernacular, Billy Wilder's *Sunset Blvd.* is still dark and unsettling, a Hollywood horror story about the worst sin a screen actress can commit—getting older. If Norma is a monster, she's like Frankenstein or King Kong in that she has our sympathies all the way. Even if she's deluded, at least she was once great and still has some semblance of talent (her Chaplin impersonation is dead-on). Joe, for all his contempt for her disconnection with reality, is and always was a hack. And while gay audiences have always enjoyed Swanson's diva posturing in this classic, it's the character of Joe I find more interesting with each viewing. There are compelling stories to be told about sugar daddies and their kept boys (in any gender match-up you please), but few films have addressed them. And besides, every time you hear about some past-her-prime starlet shacking up with a young stud, doesn't he usually wind up being at least a little on the queer side? Think about it. (Oh, and please, avoid the Andrew Lloyd Webber stage musical with every fiber of your being. It's for your own good.)

Quotes to Remember:

> **Joe:** You're Norma Desmond! You used to be in silent pictures. You used to be big!
> **Norma:** I am big! It's the pictures that got small.

> **Joe** (to Betty, about Norma): It's lonely here, so she got herself a companion. Very simple setup. Older woman who's well-to-do. Younger man who's not doing too well. Can you figure it out yourself?

See Also:

Queen Kelly (1929), in which Von Stroheim really did direct Swanson, is featured in a clip here as one of Norma's movies. And to see Von Stroheim at his peak as a great filmmaker, check out his 1924 classic *Greed*.

SWOON

(1992)

Written by Tom Kalin;
collaborating writer, Hilton Als.
Directed by Tom Kalin.
Craig Chester, Daniel Schlachet, Ron Vawter, Michael Kirby.
(Strand Releasing Home Video)

I n 1924, rich Jewish college students Nathan Leopold (Chester) and Richard Loeb (Schlachet) shock the world with their thrill-kill murder of Bobby Franks. The two traded sexual favors for each other's involvement in petty misdemeanors, and they hoped their fake kidnapping of Franks would be a perfect crime. Much is made about their "unnatural lusts" at the trial, and both are sent to prison. Loeb is murdered by a fellow prisoner who wanted to have sex with him, although the media depicts Loeb as the aggressor. Leopold is eventually released and goes to Puerto Rico, where he spends the rest of his life with his wife and children.

★ ★

The Leopold and Loeb case was the "trial of the century." Of its decade. It inspired two previous films, Alfred Hitchcock's *Rope* (1948) and Richard Fleischer's *Compulsion* (1959), the latter based on the novel by Meyer Levin. But writer-director Kalin, who had spent most of his life fascinated by the case, set out to reclaim the infamous "Dickie" (Loeb) and "Babe" (Leopold). While their homosexuality was addressed fleetingly (and with obvious repugnance) in earlier versions, Kalin brought

Daniel Schlachet (Richard Loeb) and Craig Chester (Nathan Leopold)

their intimate relationship to the forefront while also examining how, for 1920s America, *murderer* wasn't that far adrift from the response people already had to *Jewish* and *queer*. Aggressively stylish from its creamy black-and-white cinematography to its blatant anachronisms—Walkmans, touch-tone phones—*Swoon* is a sexy and haunting portrait of bad behavior.

Quotes to Remember:

Richard (to Nathan): You want to get caught, don't you? If you could get pregnant, you would, wouldn't you?

TARNATION

(2004)

Directed by Jonathan Caouette.
Jonathan Caouette, Renee LeBlanc, Adolph Davis,
Rosemary Davis, David Sanin Paz. (Wellspring Home Video)

This powerful documentary features lifelong autochroni-
cler Caouette telling his story of growing up with a
mother made mentally ill from the series of shock therapy treatments forced upon her by her parents during
childhood and early adulthood.

★ ★

Francis Coppola once said that the proliferation of inexpen-
sive video cameras and editing equipment meant that one day, a
13-year-old fat girl in Ohio would make the great American
movie. While the young teen girls have yet to emerge as a new
artistic force, the accessibility of moviemaking tools has given us
Tarnation, a one-of-a-kind personal documentary. Created with
Apple's iMovie program, the film includes film clips of its director dating back to when he was 11. Caouette's story is a gut-
wrenching one, from his mother's suffering to his own battles
with drugs and mental illness. But it's not all horror—we see
teenage Jonathan direct his high school's musical production of
David Lynch's *Blue Velvet*, featuring songs by Marianne
Faithfull. We meet his boyfriend, David, who provides a much-
needed island of sanity. And we see Jonathan being there for his
mother, Renee, no matter how bad things get. Caouette had submitted some of this footage to John Cameron Mitchell as an

audition for one of Mitchell's film projects; Mitchell and Gus Van Sant were so taken with the material that they encouraged Caouette to turn his hours and hours of footage into a feature, which he was able to complete for less than $300. (Much more was spent, obviously, to get it ready for theatrical release.) Some critics found the film powerful, while others accuse Caouette of self-indulgence. But *Tarnation* packs a punch. It also heralds a new generation of cinema.

Aa

TAXI ZUM KLO

(1981)

Written and directed by Frank Ripploh.
Frank Ripploh, Bernd Broaderup, Orpha Termin, Peter Fahrni.
(Cinevista Home Video)

Schoolteacher Frank (Ripploh) invites us to join him on his adventures, which include sex in public restrooms, sex in public parks, and cruising pretty much every gay guy who crosses his path. He and Bernd (Broaderup) make a go at a relationship, but Frank's not into the whole not-banging-every-dude-in-sight part. After Frank shows up at school still dressed in drag from a gay ball he attended the night before, he decides to leave teaching behind and become a film-maker.

★ ★

Few films have been so flagrantly "my life and welcome to it" the way this controversial gay German feature is. It seems hard to believe that writer-director-star Ripploh could get laid as often in real life as he does in this movie and still have time to be a filmmaker, but *Taxi*, like *Prick Up Your Ears* (p. 167), captures the thrill and exhilaration of the hunt for quick pick-ups. What's perhaps most interesting about the film is its lack of judgment for or against its protagonist's behavior—you don't get the expected ending where he realizes that he's got to change his life and start comporting himself in a more heteronormative way. But at the same time, it's hard to defend his behavior when he ducks out of a hospital, where he's being treated for hepatitis, and takes a cab to a public lavatory to go cruising. (The film's title translates to *Taxi to the Toilet*, incidentally.)

TONGUES UNTIED

(1990)

Directed by Marlon Riggs.
Marlon Riggs, Essex Hemphill.
(VHS only; Strand Releasing Home Video)

Riggs's personal documentary tells his own story of struggle as a gay black man, feeling like an outsider in both worlds. Through poetry, music, and the stories of other gay black men, they express themselves openly and declare that "Black men loving black men is the revolutionary act."

★ ★

There are some films that are important to the history of cinema that you nonetheless want to watch once and then never again. But other films that make an impact can actually be entertaining. *Tongues Untied* goes into the latter category. It was one of the first movies to explore the point of view of growing up and living as a black gay man in contemporary America, but it's a movie that overflows with vitality, joy, pathos, and hope. Don't let the word "poetry" put you off—*Tongues* never feels ponderous or arty. Riggs has the talent of making his stories both universal and specific in their immediacy, and noted queer poet Essex Hemphill is sexy, dynamic, and moving performing his own works. While the film is very much a snapshot of its specific time, *Tongues Untied* continues to speak to divisions that separate the black and queer communities in this country.

AUTEUR ALERT:

While Riggs's very promising career was cut short by complications due to AIDS, he made a fascinating collection of documentaries, including *Black Is...Black Ain't* (1994) and a study of blacks on prime-time TV, *Color Adjustment* (1991). Karen Everett's 1996 *I Shall Not Be Removed: The Life of Marlon Riggs* examines the life and work of this amazing artist.

See Also:

Released around the same time as *Tongues Untied*, Isaac Julien's *Looking for Langston* (1988) also beautifully explores issues surrounding blackness and gayness.

TRICK

(1999)

Written by Jason Schafer.
Directed by Jim Fall.
Christian Campbell, J.P. Pitoc, Tori Spelling,
Clinton Leupp, Kate Flannery. (New Line Home Video)

Frustrated composer Gabriel (Campbell) flirts with hunky go-go boy Mark (Pitoc) on the subway, but finding a place to consummate their attraction proves terribly difficult, what with Gabriel's straight roommate taking over their pad to sleep with his girlfriend, who's just back from Paris. The two go to a muscle-guy dance club, where gym-bunny lugs hit on Mark while Gabriel is trapped in the bathroom by a vengeful drag queen (Leupp). Gabriel and Mark go out for breakfast but are set upon by Gabriel's friend Katherine (Spelling) and her theater pals. But while they never get to have sex, they might fall in love instead.

★ ★

By the end of the 1990s there was no shortage of frothy and disposable gay romantic comedies. So why does *Trick* still stand out as a gem? For one thing, Jason Schafer's sprightly screenplay keeps the action moving, stopping here and there to give us some character depth and oddball supporting players. Next, there's the utter charm of Campbell and Pitoc in the lead roles—in real life, of course, guys who look like Pitoc generally hook up with other guys who look like Pitoc. But what's a rom-com without an element of fantasy? When these two get their big kiss at the end, it feels earned and even cathartic, in the way that great movie kisses do. Tori Spelling's comedic work here was a revelation—her third-act meltdown will make you forgive her for *Beverly Hills 90210* and even for *Coed Call Girl*—and Leupp gives us a taste of the comic chops he would get to unleash at greater lengths in *Girls Will Be Girls* (p. 90).

Quotes to Remember:

Barfly: What do you do?

Gabriel: What do I do? Writer.

Barfly: What do you write?

Gabriel: Musicals. I feel really lame telling people that because it makes me seem like a queen. Which I don't think I am. But it wouldn't matter if I was, anyway. Except I'm not.

Barfly: You got a boyfriend?

Gabriel: No. Would I be here if I had a boyfriend?

Barfly: I've got one.

Gabriel: Really? And where is he?

Barfly: He's at home. You want to come over? We don't live far from here.

Gabriel: Uh...I think I see a friend.

UNZIPPED

(1995)

Directed by Douglas Keeve.
Isaac Mizrahi, Sandra Bernhard, Mark Morris,
Naomi Campbell, Linda Evangelista, Eartha Kitt.
(Miramax Home Entertainment)

This documentary follows fashion designer Isaac Mizrahi as he puts together his fall 1994 collection. He's just come off an unsuccessful showing, so this new line is crucial. As we see him create clothes from his inspirations—which, for this collection, range from *Nanook of the North* (1922) to The Banana Splits—we see Isaac deal with models, meet with admirers like Eartha Kitt and Polly Mellen, hang out with Sandra Bernhard and Mark Morris, and quote liberally from *Valley of the Dolls* (see p. 216) and *What Ever Happened to Baby Jane?* (see p. 226). Finally, after countless conniptions, his fashion show is a huge smash.

★ ★

It's hard to capture what it is that's so damn fun about *Unzipped*, except to say that it's like spending 73 minutes with the world's greatest brunch guest. Mizrahi is a whirligig of inspiration and creativity, and while he's probably exhausting to be around in real life, it's fun to get a taste of his life in this documentary, directed by the designer's then-boyfriend. Mizrahi is a role model for anyone who grew up fey and design-minded, and his success here feels like a kind of exquisite revenge for homos everywhere. For fans of fashion, there are the gorgeous clothes, and the struggle that goes into creating them. And if you love supermodels, the Mizrahi show at the end is like a perfect storm of "it girls"—Cindy! Naomi! Linda! Kate! Shalom! Veronica! If you're pining for something to watch in between seasons of *Project Runway* or *America's Next Top Model*, here's a movie for you.

Quotes to Remember:

> **Isaac:** Because I'm American. And I'm not a stone. That's why I like Mary Tyler Moore. Basically because between her and Jackie Kennedy, they shaped this country.

VALLEY OF THE DOLLS

(1967)

Written by Helen Deutsch and Dorothy Kingsley,
based on the novel by Jacqueline Susann.
Directed by Mark Robson.
Patty Duke, Barbara Parkins, Sharon Tate,
Susan Hayward, Paul Burke, Tony Scotti,
Martin Milner, Alex Davion, Lee Grant.
(Shockingly, VHS only; Twentieth Century Fox Home Entertainment)

Three young women get chewed up and spit out by show business. Anne (Parkins) goes from secretary to TV spokesmodel for a cosmetics company. Neely (Duke) climbs out of the chorus and becomes a big movie star and singing sensation. Jennifer (Tate) gets to leave her days as a stage bimbo behind her when she marries singer Tony (Scotti). But they're all doomed: Jennifer has to star in French nudies to pay the sanitarium bills for Tony, who's lost his marbles, before she's stricken with breast cancer. Neely loses two husbands— nice guy Mel (Milner) and bitchy fashion designer Ted (Davion)—and her movie career over her many addictions. And Anne loses Lyon (Burke), the love of her life, when he betrays her with boozy pillhead Neely.

Patty Duke (Neely O'Hara)

★ ★

The cornerstone of camp cinema, this hit adaptation of Jacqueline Susann's runaway best-seller remains one of Hollywood's trashiest howlers. "You've got to climb Mount Everest to reach the Valley of the Dolls," says Parkins at the beginning of the film, and *VOD* remains on that exclusive peak with *Mommie Dearest* (see p. 147) and a handful of other glorious misfires. From the endlessly risible dialogue ("French subtitles over a bare bottom doesn't necessarily make it art") to the can-you-believe-they-left-this-in bloopers (watch Patty Duke's necklace during the telethon scene), *VOD* offers laughs aplenty.

Fun facts:

★ Part of the notoriety of Susann's novel stems from the fact that her characters are all loosely based on real showbiz figures. Neely is really Judy Garland, Jennifer is starlet Carole Landis,

Broadway gorgon Helen Lawson (Hayward) is modeled after Ethel Merman, and Anne is supposed to represent Susann herself, who found semi-fame as a model on early TV commercials and was once voted the "best-dressed woman on television."

★ Despite the fact that her tragic life and career were the basis of one of the book's characters, Judy Garland originally signed on to play Helen Lawson and made it through costume tests and one disastrous day of shooting. On the second day, she was fired, but she did manage to take her outfits with her and wore at least one of them in her stage act.

★ *The Hollywood Reporter* said at one point that Candice Bergen, Petula Clark, and Raquel Welch were set to play the film's leads. And novelist Harlan Ellison wrote an early script outline before being replaced.

★ Patty Duke later wrote about on-set tension in her memoir *Call Me Anna* (cowritten with Kenneth Turan), finally noting, "I hated [director] Mark Robson. I truly hated that man."

Quotes to Remember:

[Neely walks into the ladies' room at a party, only to find her longtime rival Helen there]

Neely: Who ya hidin' from, Helen? The notices couldn't have been that bad.

Helen: The show just needs a little doctoring.

Neely: Well, if it flops, you can always be understudy for my grandmother.

Helen: Thanks! I've already turned down the role you're playing.

Neely: Bull! Merrick's not that crazy.

Helen: You should know, honey. You just came out of a nuthouse.

Neely: It was not a nuthouse!

Helen: Look—they drummed you out of Hollywood. So now you come crawling back to Broadway. Well Broadway doesn't go for booze and dope. Now you get out of my way, I got a man waitin' for me.

Neely: That's a switch from the fags you're usually stuck with.

Helen: At least I never married one!

Neely: You take that back! [Wig-pulling catfight ensues]

Neely: Suit yourself. I'm too tired to argue. I'm gonna take a shower and get back to Ted Casablanca's.

Mel: You know, you're spending a lot more time than necessary with that fag.

Neely: Ted Casablanca is not a fag! And I'm the dame who can prove it.

VICTIM

(1961)

Written by Janet Green and John McCormick.
Directed by Basil Dearden.
Dirk Bogarde, Sylvia Sims, Dennis Price, Anthony Nicholls.
(Home Vision Entertainment)

Respected London barrister Melville Farr (Bogarde) begins investigating a blackmail ring after a young friend, Jack Barrett, kills himself. Because homosexuality itself was a crime in Great Britain, gay men in earlier eras were extremely vulnerable to blackmail. As Farr gets deeper into the investigation, his wife, Laura (Sims), realizes that he was in love with Barrett. Farr commits himself to tracking down the blackmailers, even if it means the destruction of his own reputation.

★ ★

All these decades later and *Victim* remains a riveting look at a much more repressive time in gay history. Stranger still, however, is how relevant the film has remained. While a married big-shot barrister like Farr could easily come out of the closet and still have a career in today's London, out gay men are still trying to convince closeted celebrities to stop lying about their lives. (See Quotes to Remember, below.) For a 1961 movie to take on an established law against an unpopular subset of the population—and for a big star like Bogarde to have played the lead role—was a huge deal. But while *Victim* is clearly a movie with an agenda, it's still an entertaining sit. Those of you who are fuzzy about Stonewall, let alone anything that happened before that historical turning point in the gay rights movement, should definitely pop this one in and let it blow your mind.

Quotes to Remember:

Detective Inspector Harris: Whatever the blackmailers had on Barrett concerns Farr, of that I'm certain.
Bridie: But Farr's married, sir.
Harris: Those are famous last words, Bridie.

Henry: I can't help the way I am, but the law says I'm a criminal. I've been to prison four times. Couldn't go through that again, not at my age. I'm going to Canada. I've made up my mind to be "sensible," as the prison doctor used to say. Who'll care how lonely...but sensible. Nature played me a dirty trick. I'm going to see I get a few years' peace and quiet in return. Tell them there's no magic cure for who we are, certainly not behind prison bars.

Laura: I thought you loved me. If you do, what did you feel for him? I have a right to know.
Farr: All right, you want to know. I shall tell you. You won't be content until you know, will you? Until you've ripped it out of me! I stopped seeing him because I wanted him. Do you understand? I *wanted* him! Now what good has that done you?

Calloway [a famous theater actor]: I've never corrupted the normal. Why should I be forced to live outside the law because I find love in the only way I can?
Farr: You're a star, Calloway. People like you set a fashion. If the young people knew how you lived, mightn't that be an example to follow?

Harris: Somebody once called this law against homosexuals "the blackmailer's charter."
Farr: Is that how you feel about it?
Harris: I'm a policeman, sir. I don't have feelings.

VICTOR/
VICTORIA

(1982)

Written by Blake Edwards,
based on the film *Viktor und Viktoria*, written by Reinhold Schünzel.
Directed by Blake Edwards.
Julie Andrews, Robert Preston, James Garner, Lesley Anne Warren,
Alex Karras, John Rhys-Davies, Graham Stark.
(MGM Home Entertainment)

Destitute soprano Victoria (Andrews) is sheltered by gay cabaret singer Toddy (Preston), who hatches a brilliant scheme: They will pass Victoria off as Count Victor Grezhinski, Poland's greatest female impersonator. "Victor" becomes the toast of 1930s Paris and catches the eye of visiting Chicago nightclub owner King Marchand (Garner), who is perturbed to find himself attracted to this Polish gentleman. King finds out Victoria is really a woman, but seeing King and "Victor" in bed together compels King's bodyguard Squash (Karras) to come out of the closet and bed down with Toddy. King has a hard time pretending to be involved with a man, but when his screechy ex-girlfriend Norma (Warren) comes to town with some homophobic Chicago mobsters, all is revealed.

★ ★

A perfect marriage between writer-director Blake Edwards's gift for farce and physical comedy, some charming Henry

Mancini songs, and a cast of great comic performers resulted in this delightful comedy. OK, yes, there are some areas where it could be bolder—for one thing, the movie goes well out of its way to let King ascertain that "Victor" is indeed a woman before the two kiss. (King says, "I don't care if you *are* a man" before they smooch, so it's too bad the film doesn't have the courage to make that line be true.) And Preston's Toddy, while a wonderful character, is just a bit too late-20th-century in his forthright gayness. But these are minor quibbles—*Victor/Victoria* is a total treat.

Quotes to Remember:

Toddy (responding to applause at a gay bar): Thank you. You're most kind. In fact, you're every kind.

Victoria: How long have you been a homosexual?
Toddy: How long have you been a soprano?
Victoria: Since I was 12.
Toddy: I was a late bloomer.

Victoria: Toddy, I don't know how to act like a man.
Toddy: Contrary to the popular conception of how a man acts, there are all sorts of men who act in all sorts of ways.
Victoria: I mean, as opposed to the way women act.
Toddy: I am personally acquainted with at least a dozen men who act exactly like women, and vice versa.
Victoria: But there are just some things that are naturally masculine.
Toddy: Name one.
Victoria: Uh...peeing standing up.
Toddy: [Laughs] On the other hand, there's absolutely no rule that says a man can't sit down.

Norma: You know what I think?

Toddy: What?

Norma: I think that the right woman could reform you.

Toddy: You know, I think the right woman could reform you too.

Norma: [*Squeals*] Me, give up men? Forget it!

Toddy: You took the words right out of my mouth.

King: How long...I mean, exactly when did you know about...

Squash: When did I know I was gay?

King: Yeah.

Squash: God, I can't remember when I wasn't.

King: I've known you for 15 years!

Squash: Well, you know a lot of guys, boss. You'd be surprised.

King: You were an all-American. I never saw a meaner, rougher, tougher, son-of-a-bitch football player in all my life.

Squash: Listen, if you didn't want the guys to call you queer, you became a rough, tough, son-of-a-bitching football player.

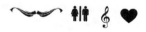

WHAT EVER HAPPENED TO BABY JANE?

(1962)

Written by Lukas Heller,
based on the novel by Henry Farrell.
Directed by Robert Aldrich.
Bette Davis, Joan Crawford, Victor Buono,
Wesley Addy, Marjorie Bennett. (Warner Home Video)

Former vaudeville star Baby Jane Hudson (Davis) lives in a modest Los Angeles home, taking care of her invalid sister, former Hollywood star Blanche Hudson (Crawford). While Blanche resented her sister's success when they were children, she took care of her in their adult years, insisting at the height of her fame that the studio make a film with Jane for every one they made with Blanche. One night, after a party where Jane was drunk, there was a terrible car accident that left Blanche crippled and wheelchair-bound. Years later Jane is an alcoholic who still grotesquely dresses like a little girl, and Blanche wants to sell the house and put Jane away.

Jane begins torturing Blanche while attempting a comeback. But Blanche may not be the blameless victim she appears to be.

★ ★

While modern audiences can no longer experience the shock that 1962 moviegoers must have felt in seeing glamorous Hollywood legends Davis and Crawford playing old, ugly, and twisted characters, *Baby Jane* still packs a rather visceral punch. For one thing, gay gossips know just how much Davis and Crawford always hated each other offscreen, so watching them humiliate and abuse each other in their only costarring film is always a hoot. The film's cruelty is both repellent and fascinating; fans of *Mommie Dearest* (p. 147) will particularly enjoy seeing Crawford victimized in light of allegations about her real-life parenting. Any drag queen who does Bette Davis is bound to have at least one line from this film in his repertoire.

Fun facts:

★ "Bert Hanley," the Hudson sisters' discussed-but-never-seen business manager, is also the name of the drunken composer in *Camp* (see p. 40).

★ Screenwriter Heller and director Aldrich collaborated on another film about an aging actress—*The Killing of Sister George* (see p. 120).

★ The movie footage we see of the Hudson sisters comes from real Joan Crawford and Bette Davis films—the movie Blanche watches on television is *Sadie McKee* (1934), while Jane's bad acting comes from an early Davis vehicle called *Parachute Jumper* (1933).

★ There was a 1991 made-for-TV remake, starring the Redgrave sisters, Vanessa (Blanche) and Lynn (Jane). It can't hold a candle to the original, but it's worth TiVoing off cable in the middle of the night if you get the chance.

Quote to Remember:

> **Blanche:** You wouldn't be able to do these awful things to me if I weren't still in this chair!
>
> **Jane:** But ya are, Blanche! Ya *are* in that chair!

WILLY WONKA & THE CHOCOLATE FACTORY

(1971)

Written by Roald Dahl
(and an uncredited David Seltzer),
based on Dahl's novel *Charlie and the Chocolate Factory*.
Directed by Mel Stuart.
Gene Wilder, Peter Ostrum, Jack Albertson,
Roy Kinnear, Julie Dawn Cole, Denise Nickerson,
Dodo Denney. (Warner Home Video)

A fey bachelor (Wilder) with a devilish sense of humor and a talent for confections invites five children from around the world to tour his amazing chocolate factory. He booby-traps the tour with moral challenges that the children are all destined to fail, and they do, one by one, falling prey to the deadly tortures of the "Candy Man." Eventually, an impoverished child (Ostrum) outsmarts the snares, and he earns the right to become the older man's protégé. He will be groomed to take over the cloistered, all-male empire.

★ ★

Just kidding. *Willy Wonka & the Chocolate Factory* endures as both wonderful children's entertainment and a movie that amuses adults who can't believe that such a dark, twisted film can get away with being wonderful children's entertainment. This is the rare movie that doesn't pander to kids—yes, little ones, the world *is* a creepy and scary and unsettling place— while also reminding them that life contains enchantment as well as horrors. And what makes this film a gay must-see, besides its dark humor and warped look at the world? It gives us the walking id known as Veruca Salt (Cole), whose mantra of "Daddy, I want it *now!*" lives on in gay circles everywhere. (And please, let's not even talk about the misguided 2005 remake.)

WITHOUT YOU I'M NOTHING

(1990)

Written by Sandra Bernhard and John Boskovich.
Directed by John Boskovich.
Sandra Bernhard. (MGM Home Entertainment)

After becoming the toast of New York with her "smash hit one-woman show," Sandra Bernhard returns to Los Angeles and performs at an upscale supper club where the audience ignores her. She reminisces about her childhood, dreams of celebrating Christmas as part of a gentile family, and talks about buying a Navajo blanket at the Andy Warhol auction. She sings songs by Nina Simone, Sylvester, and Burt Bacharach. The last remaining audience member gives her a succinct review.

★ ★

Queer entertainer Sandra Bernhard is a fucking genius. When you see her perform live, she can take a hoary and ridiculous song like "Don't Stop Believin'" or "Beautiful" and simultaneously take the piss out of it and reclaim its anthemic power. She does that to herself in *Without You I'm Nothing*, the screen version of her hit 1988 off-Broadway show. Rather than do a tra-

ditional concert film of an artist performing in front of an adoring throng—and if you listen to the cast album of *Without You*,
you'll hear a throng that's plenty adoring—Bernhard and her
collaborator John Boskovich stage her show in front of an audience of extras who have been hired to ignore or be aghast at her.
Nonetheless, her material remains brilliantly funny, whether
she's skewering marry-the-boss fantasies or documenting a
straight asshole's first trip to a gay bar. ("Somebody hands you a
tambourine!") It's performance art and social commentary and
gut-bustingly hilarious comedy in one package. Some gay men
worship at the altars of Cher, Barbra, Judy, Bette, Björk, or
Madonna, but ever since *Without You I'm Nothing*, I've been all
about Sandra.

Quote to Remember:

Sandra: My father's a proctologist; my mother's an abstract
artist. That's how I view the world.

THE WOMEN

(1939)

Written by Anita Loos and Jane Murfin,
from the play by Clare Boothe Luce.
Directed by George Cukor.
Norma Shearer, Joan Crawford, Rosalind Russell,
Mary Boland, Paulette Goddard, Phyllis Povah,
Joan Fontaine, Marjorie Main. (Warner Home Video)

Society wife Mary Haines (Shearer) discovers that her husband has been cheating on her with scheming shopgirl Crystal Allen (Crawford). Mary tries to overlook the whole thing to protect her marriage and her daughter, but her buttinsky pals (led by Russell as gossipy gorgon Sylvia Fowler) push her into seeking divorce. Two years after she and her husband split up, Mary discovers that Crystal—now married to Mary's ex—is having an affair of her own, and Mary decides that she, too, can play the gossip game to break up a marriage.

★ ★

I'll leave it to the women's studies majors to decide whether or not this story of women backbiting and undermining each other is misogynistic or not. But gay director George Cukor's comedy—famously featuring an all-female cast—has been embraced for decades by Gays of a Certain Age. While I don't love the movie as much as a lot of fags (of varying ages) I know, it's still banter-rific and loaded to the gills with fun performances, particularly Russell's and Crawford's. (Crawford so rarely got the chance to be funny. *Intentionally* funny, anyway.) Shearer's Great Lady routine has always worked my nerves, but perhaps she felt it necessary to act that way as "Queen of MGM." (When *The Women* was made, she had been recently widowed by the studio's head of production Irving Thalberg.) And if a film packed with overdressed and bitchy women didn't make this appealing enough to gay audiences, there's even Marjorie "Ma Kettle" Main dyking around for good measure.

Quotes to Remember:

Sylvia: I'm on to my husband. I wouldn't trust him on Alcatraz.

Mary's mother: Living alone has its compensations. Heaven knows, it's marvelous to be able to spread out in bed like a swastika.

Sylvia: Oh, you remember the awful things they said about what's-her-name before she jumped out the window? There. You see? I can't even remember her name so who cares?

Crystal: There's a name for you ladies, but it isn't used in high society, outside of a kennel.

See Also:

I've always had a soft spot for MGM's somewhat misguided remake of *The Women*, 1956's *The Opposite Sex*. Adding men, music, and Metrocolor was probably entirely unnecessary, but this is the version of the story I saw first, so it's stuck with me anyway. June Allyson is no less annoying than Shearer, and Joan Collins doesn't quite reach Crawford's heights, but Dolores Gray gives Russell some vivid competition as Sylvia. The original film wisely never shows us the man that Shearer and Crawford are fighting over; this version has Allyson and Collins duking it out over *Leslie Nielsen*!

WOMEN
IN
LOVE

(1969)

Written by Larry Kramer,
from the novel by D.H. Lawrence.
Directed by Ken Russell.
Glenda Jackson, Oliver Reed, Alan Bates, Jennie Linden,
Eleanor Bron, Vladek Sheybal. (MGM Home Entertainment)

I n post-World War I England, two sisters fall in love: artist Gudrun (Jackson) with brash industrialist Gerald (Reed), and teacher Ursula (Linden) with schools inspector Rupert (Bates). Following a conversation about male friendship, Gerald and Rupert strip naked and wrestle in front of a roaring fireplace. The four travel together to Switzerland after Ursula and Rupert marry; Gudrun has an affair with a bisexual sculptor (Sheybal). After nearly killing Gudrun and her lover, Gerald wanders off into the snow.

★ ★

This brilliant adaptation of the D.H. Lawrence classic marks Kramer's transition from studio executive to writer. Following his acclaim (including an Oscar nomination) for this film, he went on to write the landmark AIDS play *The Normal Heart* and to become one of history's most influential queer activists. (Oddly enough, it was the fat paycheck he earned for writing the treacly 1973 musical remake of *Lost Horizon* that allowed him to leave Hollywood behind and support himself as a playwright, essayist, and activist. Who knew closeted megaproducer Ross Hunter [*Imitation of Life* (1959), *Airport* (1970)] would accidentally become a hero of the gay rights movement?) There's a lot to say about *Women in Love*, and how it's one of Ken Russell's most restrained and powerful movies, but let's cut to the chase: That wrestling scene between Bates and Reed is one of the sexiest things ever committed to film. Even as films got more explicit and pornography came out from the underground, there's still never been anything else like it before or since. Check it out.

Quotes to Remember:

> **Rupert:** The proper way to eat a fig in society is to split it in four, holding it by the stump, and open it so that it is a glittering, rosy, moist, honeyed heavy-petalled flower. Then you throw away the skin after you have taken off the blossom with your lips. But the vulgar way is just to put your mouth to the crack and take out the flesh in one bite. The fig is a very secretive fruit. The Italians vulgarly say it stands for the female part, the fig fruit, the fissure, the yoni, the wonderful moist conductivity towards the center...involved, in-turned. One small way of access only, and this close-curtained from the light. Sap that smells strange on your fingers, so that even goats won't taste it. And when the fig has kept her secret long enough, so it explodes, and you see through the fissure the scarlet. And the fig is finished, the year is over. That's how the fig dies, showing her crimson through the purple slit like a wound, the exposure of her secret on the open day. Like a prostitute, the bursten fig makes a show of her secret.

 **Aa** ≡

WRITTEN ON THE WIND

(1956)

Written by George Zuckerman,
from the novel by Robert Wilder.
Directed by Douglas Sirk.
Rock Hudson, Lauren Bacall, Robert Stack, Dorothy Malone,
Robert Keith, Grant Williams. (Criterion Collection)

Secretary Lucy Moore (Bacall) marries millionaire Kyle Hadley (Stack). Kyle has been a failure all his life, rescued from scrapes by his working-class best friend Mitch Wayne (Hudson). Mitch loves Lucy, but says nothing about it. Kyle's sister Marylee (Malone) resents him for taking away her childhood sweetheart, Mitch, who loves her only as a sister. Kyle starts drinking again when he thinks he is infertile. When Lucy manages to get pregnant, Marylee goads Kyle into thinking Lucy and Mitch have had an affair. After Kyle and Mitch have an altercation, Kyle is shot. Evidence suggests that Mitch is the killer, but Marylee tearfully admits at the inquest that she struggled with Kyle, and the gun went off. Mitch and Lucy leave Marylee alone with her fortune and her regrets.

★ ★

Sometimes it's tricky to distinguish between art and camp. The first time I saw *Written on the Wind*, in a college film class, I laughed all the way through it. Here's a movie where a man who's just been told he might be impotent walks outside and sees a boy bouncing up and down on a hobby horse. Where a woman *mambos her father to death*, for heaven's sake. In later years, I've read enough about Douglas Sirk and the power of the melodrama to appreciate this movie as a film classic. But damn, it's still kind of ridiculous. Malone is nothing but awesome here—she won a well-deserved Oscar—but she's called upon to do a lot of pouting and chest-heaving and to drool over Rock Hudson like he's a piece of meat (her confusion is completely understandable). The movie's opening credits feature more looking-through-curtains-with-intent than the entire run of most TV soap operas; and the ending features a forlorn Malone sitting at her father's desk and hugging his, um, *oil well*. (OK, it's a miniature replica of one, but *still*. I mentioned that she mambos him to death, right?) So watch this film as a stirring examination of one rich family's decadent rot or as a laughably overstuffed weepie. Either way, you'll be utterly entertained.

Quotes to Remember:

>**Kyle:** Cream?
>**Lucy:** I never use it.
>**Kyle:** Shows how little I know you.

>**Kyle:** You're a filthy liar.
>**Marylee:** I'm filthy. Period!

XANADU

(1980)

Written by Richard Christian Danus and Marc Reid Rubel.
Directed by Robert Greenwald.
Olivia Newton-John, Gene Kelly, Michael Beck.
(Universal Home Video)

When Sonny (Beck) gives up his dream of being an artist, he summons forth the nine Muses from a mural at the beach in Southern California. Terpsichore, calling herself Kira (Newton-John), roller-skates into his life and convinces him and retired big band leader Danny McGuire (Kelly) to open a dazzling roller-disco palace called Xanadu.

★ ★

Olivia Newton-John was apparently such a hot item at the box office after the amazing success of *Grease* (1978) that producers must have figured they could stick her in anything, and audiences would show up. Apparently "anything" didn't include a roller-disco remake of *Down to Earth* (1947) featuring a not-exactly-in-his-prime Gene Kelly and the—let's face it—kinda creepy star of *The Warriors* (1979). (The movie's supposed to be a romance between Beck and Newton-John, but he's got way more chemistry with Kelly.) But even if *Xanadu* was a dud in 1980, the movie definitely has a fervent cult today. Half of that following are wide-eyed true believers who love it and think time has been kind to it; the other half laugh at the inane script and severely dated hair and wardrobe choices. I tend to fall into the latter camp, but I can relate to the former as well: Even in his late 60s, Kelly could still cut a rug with the best of them, and it's exciting to watch him duet with Newton-John on "Whenever You're Away from Me." And even if the choreography is often silly and the leg warmers become overbearing, there's no denying that the Olivia Newton-John and ELO songs are all pretty terrific. All of which is to say that *Xanadu* is pretty much a piece of crap, but you'll find yourself wanting to watch it again and again anyway.

Quote to Remember:

[After Danny tells Sonny he wants him to own half of Xanadu]
Sonny: I don't know the first thing about being a partner.
Danny: It's easy. We share the responsibilities, and we argue a lot. It's like being married...without the good part.

ZERO PATIENCE

(1993)

Written and directed by John Greyson.
John Robinson, Normand Fauteux, Dianne Heatherington,
Richardo Keens-Douglas, Michael Callen.
(Strand Releasing Home Video)

P atient Zero (Fauteux), accused by many of bringing
AIDS to North America, returns to earth from limbo
when Sir Richard Burton (Robinson)—immortal after
finding the Fountain of Youth—plans to feature Zero in
a "Hall of Contagion" museum exhibit. Burton meets and falls in
love with Zero, learning that he was wrong to think of the notorious flight attendant as some kind of serial killer. Further
research shows Burton that Zero probably wasn't the first person—or at least not the only person—on the continent with the
virus, and that many of Burton's AIDS scapegoats, from the
African green monkey to HIV itself, may be more innocent than
he had originally thought.

★ ★

Much as he had done in his earlier film *Urinal* (1998)—
which gathered Langston Hughes, Yukio Mishima, and Frida
Kahlo in modern-day Toronto to discuss the ethics of gay sex in
public restrooms—Greyson matches disparate historical characters to address certain points about blame and the culture of
empiricism as it affects the AIDS crisis. Oh, and he makes it a

David Gale, Charles Azulay, and Howard Rosenstein

musical. The real "patient zero," according to Randy Shilts's *And the Band Played On*, was a French Canadian flight attendant named Gaetan Dugas. Greyson seeks to clear his name by matching him up with repressed homosexual Burton, the explorer known for his English translations of the *Kama Sutra* and the *Arabian Nights*. Through the Victorian Burton, Greyson can attack the "culture of certainty" that seeks easy answers where none exist; in referencing the *Arabian Nights*, the director channels legendary yarn-spinner Scheherazade, keeping Patient Zero alive by telling his story and clearing his name. *Zero Patience* is a dense thicket of ideas, concepts, and musical numbers, and while it may not be consistently successful, it always gets points for trying. It's also a lot of fun. From legendary queer singer Michael Callen's cameo as a Streisand-esque "Miss HIV" to composer Glenn Schellenberg's catchy tunes in a number of genres to Burton and Zero's "Butthole Duet" (which you're just going to have to see for yourself), there's enough going on in this AIDS musical to merit more than one viewing.

AUTEUR ALERT:

Queer Canadian filmmaker Greyson's work is consistently vision-
ary, bold, and sexy. After *Zero Patience* and *Urinal*, give a look to
Lilies (1996), *Uncut* (1997), and *Proteus* (2003).

INDEX OF NAMES

D

E

H

S

INDEX
OF TITLES

INDEX OF CATEGORIES

INDEX OF CATEGORIES

**WOULD IT KILL YOU TO
WATCH A LESBIAN MOVIE?**